UNIVERSITY OF NORTH CAROLINA AT CHAPEL HILL

DEPARTMENT OF ROMANCE LANGUAGES

NORTH CAROLINA STUDIES
IN THE ROMANCE LANGUAGES AND LITERATURES

ESSAYS; TEXTS, TEXTUAL STUDIES AND TRANSLATIONS; SYMPOSIA

Founder: URBAN TIGNER HOLMES

Distributed by:

UNIVERSITY OF NORTH CAROLINA PRESS
CHAPEL HILL
North Carolina 27514
U.S.A.

NORTH CAROLINA STUDIES IN THE
ROMANCE LANGUAGES AND LITERATURES

Essays

Number 11

FIRE AND ICE:

THE POETRY OF XAVIER VILLAURRUTIA

FIRE AND ICE:
THE POETRY OF
XAVIER VILLAURRUTIA

BY

MERLIN H. FORSTER

CHAPEL HILL

NORTH CAROLINA STUDIES IN THE ROMANCE
LANGUAGES AND LITERATURES
U.N.C. DEPARTMENT OF ROMANCE LANGUAGES

1976

PQ 7297
V6 Z53

Library of Congress Cataloging in Publication Data

Forster, Merlin H.
    Fire and ice.

    (North Carolina studies in the Romance languages and literatures:
Essays; 11)
    Includes bibliographical references and index.
    1. Villaurrutia, Xavier, 1903-1950—Criticism and interpretation.
I. Title. II. Series.

PQ7297.V6Z65   868   75-29194
ISBN 0-88438-011-4

I.S.B.N. 0-88438-011-4

IMPRESO EN ESPAÑA

PRINTED IN SPAIN

DEPÓSITO LEGAL: V. 282 - 1976

ARTES GRÁFICAS SOLER, S. A. - JÁVEA, 28 - VALENCIA (8) - 1976

CONTENTS

PREFACE

Modern Mexican poetry is generally considered to be one of the most vital in the varied poetic expression of Latin America, and in recent years has received increasing attention from scholars, anthologists, and translators. At the same time, however, considerably more attention has been placed on overview and synthesis than on close internal analysis.

Xavier Villaurrutia is a major figure in the development of Mexican literature in the twentieth century, and his poetry especially is appropriate for analytical study. To begin with, there is little likelihood that the canon of his poetic works will be changed by undiscovered material, particularly in view of the rather complete 1966 compilation of his works. Also, the interplay of linguistic and conceptual elements in Villaurrutia's poetic world is of sufficient complexity to make this kind of study rewarding. Finally, a recent study in English (Frank Dauster, *Xavier Villaurrutia*, New York, Twayne, 1971) provides a general background, and makes unnecessary a detailed consideration of biography and complete works.

This work is the result of a number of years of research and study, both in this country and in Mexico, and I recognize the generous support of the faculty research and fellowship programs of the University of Illinois and of the Latin American Studies Committee of the Social Science Research Council. The Villaurrutia family in Mexico City was most kind in allowing me access to private papers and correspondence, and Dr. Elías Nandino, Alí Chumacero, Miguel Capistrán, and a host of other Mexican friends have been most helpful. John S. Brushwood read several chapters in draft, and Angelina Pietrangeli and José Emilio Pacheco read the entire manuscript;

I acknowledge gratefully their many useful observations. Finally, I am indebted to my students, whose enthusiastic and searching comments have caused me to see many things more clearly.

MHF

URBANA, ILLINOIS
May, 1973

CHAPTER I

INTRODUCTION

The Man

Xavier Villaurrutia y González was born March 27, 1903, in Mexico City, and with the exception of the greater part of a year which he spent in the United States as a fellow of the Rockefeller Foundation, he lived, wrote and died in that city. During the 1920's and 1930's he was a part of the notable group of close friends now known as the "Contemporáneos," [1] and by the time of his death in 1950 he was widely regarded as one of Mexico's leading artistic and intellectual figures.

---

[1] This name was taken from the title of the group's most important literary journal, *Contemporáneos* (1928-1931). For more information on the group and the journal, see: José Luis Martínez, *Literatura mexicana, Siglo XX* (México, Robredo, 1949), I, 29-38; Frank N. Dauster, *Breve historia de la poesía mexicana* (México, Andrea, 1956), 149-166; Luis Leal, "Torres Bodet y los 'Contemporáneos'," *Hispania,* 40 (1957), 290-296, Raúl Leiva, *Imagen de la poesía mexicana contemporánea* (México, Imprenta Universitaria, 1959), 75-190; Merlin H. Forster, "The 'Contemporáneos': A Major Group in Mexican Vanguardismo," *Texas Studies in Literature and Language,* 3 (1962), 425-438; Merlin H. Forster, "La revista *Contemporáneos*: ¿Hacia una mexicanidad universal?" *Hispanófila,* Núm. 17 (enero de 1963), 117-122; Octavio Corvalán, *Modernismo y vanguardia* (New York, Las Americas, 1967), 135-153; Edward J. Mullen, "The *Revista Contemporáneos*: A New Dimension in Contemporary Mexican Literature," *Language Quarterly,* 8 (Fall-Winter 1969), 27-31; Jean Franco, *An Introduction to Spanish American Literature* (London, Cambridge, 1969), 263-266, Edward J. Mullen, "*Contemporáneos* in Mexican Intellectual History, 1928-1931," *Journal of Inter-American Studies and World Affairs,* 13 (1971), 121-130; Edward J. Mullen, "Critical Reactions to the Review *Contemporáneos*," *Hispania,* 54 (1971), 145-149.

Villaurrutia's public life was active and varied. He took a prominent part in the theatrical world of Mexico City, taught classes at the National University, lectured widely both in the capital and in provincial cities, was an important figure in the publication of several notable literary journals, and a regular participant in several literary *tertulia* gatherings in the city. On the other hand, his private life was, as one friend has called it, "una región de sombras," not to be completely penetrated or shared even by those closest to him. He never married, but lived with his mother and younger sisters and brother in the Colonia Roma section of Mexico City. At the same time he kept a study — apartment in the downtown area and there often received friends and visitors. A person of strong but well-controlled emotions, Villaurrutia maintained both warm friendships with a number of people and strong antipathies for many others. He was one of the most cultured and widely read men of his period, with a certain interest in music and dance steps that led him to the writing of lyrics for popular songs.[2] Intensely rational and intellectual in many aspects of his life, he was also notably superstitious and obsessed by fears. A friend recalls, for example, that he once called off a planned trip to France because of a chance happening which he took to be an ill omen, and his fear of being buried alive was well known to many of his acquaintances.[3]

He was universally esteemed and feared for his penetrating caustic humor and for his amazing verbal inventiveness. Many anecdotes and epigrams which show this facet of his personality still circulate among his friends. The short stature of Alfredo Gómez de la Vega, one of the most notable Mexican actors of the day, was the target for one of Villaurrutia's mocking verses:

> La lluvia siempre acongoja
> A don Alfredo. ¿Por qué?
> Porque si Alfredo se moja,

---

[2] Elías Nandino has given me copies of a number of popular lyrics written by Villaurrutia under a pseudonym.

[3] One friend indicates that this fear was so great in Villaurrutia that he exacted a promise from several of his friends to verify his death in some absolute fashion. In deference to his request, a vein in the arm was opened just prior to the body's being removed from the catafalque in the Bellas Artes building.

Por poco que Alfredo encoja,
El público ya no lo ve. [4]

Elías Nandino, long a friend and confidant, relays the following epigram celebrating the imposing figures of two *grandes dames* of the Mexican theater, Doña Virginia Fábregas and Doña Prudencia Grifel:

Tanto han llegado a engordar
Que bien podremos decir
Virginia tarda en entrar
Lo que Prudencia en salir.

After the premiere performance of Catalina D'Erzell's new play *Maternidad*, the playwright asked that Villaurrutia say a few words from his box seat. The poet responded in this manner:

Ninguna otra concibe
Con tanta velocidad:
Que, en una noche, recibe
Estreno — y maternidad. [5]

Villaurrutia was completely unawed by important people, and took delight in reducing them to size. An interesting illustration is a story having to do with President Lázaro Cárdenas. Cárdenas had invited Villaurrutia, along with a number of other notable artists and intellectuals, to the National Palace to "exchange ideas" with him. Villaurrutia repeatedly refused to go, and at a chance meeting at a reception Cárdenas questioned Villaurrutia face to face about it. "Are you against my government's policy," asked Cárdenas, "or do you just dislike me personally?" "Neither, my dear general Cárdenas," responded Villaurrutia. "Then why didn't you accept my invitations?" demanded the President. "Well," quipped Villaurrutia, "you said that you wanted to exchange ideas, and frankly, Mr. President, that didn't strike me as a fair trade." All within earshot expected Cárdenas to react violently, but he simply responded, "You *are* intelligent, Villaurrutia! I'm flattered to be the object of one of your new epigrams." [6]

---

[4] Salvador Novo, "Xavier Villaurrutia epigramático," *México en la cultura* (12 de dic., 1965), 2.
[5] *Ibid.*
[6] This account seems somewhat elaborated, but conversations with several friends lead me to believe that at least in large part it is factual.

Fundamentally, however, Xavier Villaurrutia the man is synonomous with Xavier Villaurrutia the writer, whose complexities are not expressed primarily or even partially by humor and verbal facility. The second edition of his works (México, FCE, 1966) runs to somewhat more than a thousand pages and includes several collections of poetry, fifteen plays, a short novel, and an extensive series of essays on many topics published during his entire career. His essays brought him renown as a critic of art, literature, and the cinema, and his plays often received more public attention than those of playwrights who perhaps were superior to him. Villaurrutia enjoyed this acclaim, and took pleasure in twitting those less successful than he, as can be seen in this epigram in which he reminds Rodolfo Usigli that *Corona de sombra* had failed even before it opened:

El fracaso de Carlota
A Rodolfo lo incomoda
Y hace de bilis derroche.
Usigli, no dés la nota.
Eres el autor de moda
—Que nunca llega a la noche. [7]

In spite of his success and importance in other genres, Villaurrutia considered himself to be primarily a poet, and it is in his verses that the most genuine expression of his complex personality can be found. His production, however, is not extensive. The three main collections (*Reflejos*, 1926; *Nostalgia de la muerte*, 1938 with second edition in 1946; *Canto a la primavera y otros poemas*, 1948), together with some earlier poems and a few compositions published posthumously, constitute the material which occupies the first ninety pages of the 1966 edition of his works. The number of compositions barely exceeds one hundred, and many of these are poems of one or two stanzas. In spite of such brevity, however, Villauruttia's poems are unusually rich in imagery, and express powerfully an anguished subterranean world.

Survey of Previous Criticism on Villaurrutia

The body of critical material on Xavier Villaurrutia, not including the numerous newspaper reviews of his plays, [8] now exceeds three

---

[7] Novo, "Villaurrutia epigramático," p. 2.
[8] Based on the files of clippings that I have seen among Villaurrutia's personal papers, I would estimate that such reviews might easily run to several hundred. This material has never been fully collected or organized.

hundred titles.[9] Of these, a considerable number are brief reviews or *semblanzas* which contribute little to the serious criticism of Villaurrutia's works. There are, however, sufficient substantial studies to permit a useful three-part survey of criticism up to the present. The first of these divisions (1920-1950) encompasses those commentaries and studies which appeared up to the time of his death. The second (1951-1960) includes such important gatherings as the memorial materials shortly after his death, the first important gathering of his poetry and plays, and the first serious scholarly studies of his work. The third period (1961-1970) takes into account a number of more recent important studies and a more complete second collection of his works.

1920-1950

The critical material which appeared during Villaurrutia's own lifetime can be classified in several ways. First, there is a rather large group of critical notes and reviews which appeared in a variety of journals and other publications. These items are important in assessing the reception which Villaurrutia's works had as they were published, but none among them is sufficiently extensive or penetrating to deserve individual attention. Second, several critics identified Villaurrutia as a part of an important grouping of Mexican writers and placed him in the larger frame of twentieth-century literary development in Mexico. An early example is the panoramic article by fellow "Contemporáneo" Jaime Torres Bodet, published first under the title "Perspectiva de la literatura mexicana actual" (*Contemporáneos*, 2, núm. 4, sept. de 1928, pp. 1-33). In his well-known *Antología de la poesía española e hispanoamericana* (Madrid, Hernando, 1934), Federico de Onís has commentary and bibliography on Villaurrutia, as well as a selection of his poems. Arturo Torres Ríoseco considers Villaurrutia briefly in his article "La poesía lírica mexicana" (*El Libro y el Pueblo*, 11, 1933, pp. 204-216), but Luis Monguió's similar article, "Poetas postmodernistas mexicanos" (*Revista Hispánica Moderna*, 12, 1946, pp. 259-261) is a much more expert placing of

---

[9] The principal gatherings of these titles are the following: Luis Mario Schneider, "Bibliografía de Xavier Villaurrutia," *Obras* (Mexico, FCE, 1966), pp. lix-lxxi; *Diccionario de escritores mexicanos* (México, UNAM, 1967), s.v. "Villaurrutia, Xavier."

Villaurrutia, among others, in the literary context of his time. José Luis Martínez achieves a similar consideration and placement in his fundamental work, *Literatura mexicana, Siglo XX* (México, Robredo, 1949, I, pp. 29-38). In her unpublished thesis "Influencia de Juan Ramón Jiménez en el grupo de Contemporáneos" (Universidad Femenina Mexicana, 1949), Mercedes Pesado handles less than convincingly an important problem of influence in Villaurrutia and others of his generation, as well as presenting individual characteristics for members of the group.

Two other aspects of this early period of criticism are worthy of note here. One is the important interview of Villaurrutia conducted by José Luis Martínez and Alí Chumacero and published under the title of "Con Xavier Villaurrutia" (*Tierra Nueva* 1, no. 2, 1940, pp. 74-81). The conversation recorded here is one of the most important sources for Villaurrutia's own comments on himself, his group and his own poetry. This interview documents, for example, Villaurrutia's own expression of the primacy of his role as a poet and the importance of the influence of Heidegger. A final note is that represented by Alberto R. Lopes' short article entitled "La poesía de Xavier Villaurrutia" (*Memoria del Segundo Congreso Internacional de Catedráticos de Literatura Iberoamericana*, Berkeley and Los Angeles, 1941, pp. 251-257). This article represents the first scholarly work on the poetry of Villaurrutia, and although it is rather brief Lopes is able to establish convincingly the relationship between *Reflejos* and impressionist painting as well as to suggest the intimate expression of death and life in *Nostalgia de la muerte*.

1951-1960

In the months following Villaurrutia's death there were a number of memorial appreciations of the poet and his work, most of which are now of mere documentary interest. For example, on January 7, 1951, *El Nacional* devoted its entire Sunday supplement to Villaurrutia, and the same kind of material was published in many other newspapers and journals. As might be expected, during the remaining years of the decade criticism on Villaurrutia was much more varied and substantial. With the canon of his works now closed, critics could begin to devote themselves to the totality of his work in various genres. In 1952 Vera F. Beck published an excellent article on Villaurrutia as playwright under the title "Xavier Villaurrutia, dramaturgo moderno" (*Revista Iberoamericana*, 18, 1952, pp. 27-39), and Salvador Reyes Nevárez included in his monograph *El amor y la amistad en el mexicano* (México, 1952) a chapter entitled "La poesía amorosa de Xavier Villaurrutia" (pp. 52-58).

The year 1953 was particularly important in the criticism of Villaurrutia's work. Alí Chumacero gathered together a sizable portion of the poet's work and published it under the title *Poesía y teatro completos* (México, FCE, 1953). The volume includes a prologue, a commentary on textual sources, and a brief bibliography, all done by Chumacero. Chumacero's long introductory article (24 p.) places Villaurrutia within the "Contemporáneos" group and then discusses his poetry and plays as the products of a unique artistic sensibility within that group. The contribution made here by Chumacero, both as an editor and as a critic, is a fundamental one. Arturo Torres Ríoseco devotes a few pages to Villaurrutia in his collection *Ensayos sobre literatura latinoamericana* (Mexico, FCE, 1953, pp. 204-207), and Antonio Castro Leal includes Villaurrutia in his anthology *La poesía moderna mexicana* (México, FCE, 1953). Frank N. Dauster's doctoral dissertation, completed at Yale University in 1953 under the title of "The Literary Art of Xavier Villaurrutia" (214 p.), is an excellent piece of criticism which places Villaurrutia within his literary group and then dedicates separate chapters to the several aspects of his work. The comments on Villaurrutia as poet, critic, and translator, are particularly interesting, and the sizable bibliography, both primary and secondary, is the most extensive done up to that time. The same year Dauster published in article form an important study of the poetry of Villaurrutia ("La poesía de Xavier Villaurrutia," *Revista Iberoamericana*, 18, Sept. 1953, pp. 345-359). Dauster considers Villaurrutia's poetry in terms of his three most important collections, a distinction which many later critics have followed. Anthony W. Moreno presented in 1953 a Ph.D. dissertation at the University of Pittsburgh with the title of "Xavier Villaurrutia: The Man and his Dramas." It is very short (89 p.) and is filled with judgments and documentation which are very often both incomplete and imprecise. [10]

---

[10] An example is his handling of the question of Villaurrutia's date of birth, which he proposes to be 1906 on the basis of a personal interview with surviving members of the family (p. 3). At one point in my own work

In his monograph-sized work *Tres poetas de la soledad* (México, Robredo, 1955), Ramón Xirau includes Villaurrutia alongside José Gorostiza and Octavio Paz as representing a vital expression of solitude. The chapter on Villaurrutia is entitled "Presencia de una ausencia," and in it Xirau describes what he sees as a progressive destruction of external reality in the poetry of Villaurrutia, a dissolution which produces solitude and the obsessive representation of the themes of frustrated love and of death. Rafael Cuevas' monographic *Panorámica de las letras* includes in its third volume (México, Bellas Artes, 1956, pp. 7-53) a curious study of Villaurrutia. Cuevas has a gathering of rather vague comments on surrealism in western literature, some very brief observations on the principal collections, and a most unconvincing attempt at a kind of dialogue between the poet, represented as speaking through his poems, and the critic who listens and asks questions. Two articles appeared in 1956 in a number of *Estaciones*. The first was written by Elías Nandino as a part of a memorial to the poet on the sixth anniversary of his death ("La poesía de Xavier Villaurrutia," *Estaciones,* 1, 1956, pp. 460-468). Nandino recalls his long friendship with Villaurrutia and then traces in brief outline form the principal elements of his poetry, including also a small anthology of some of his verses. This article must be taken more as a personal expression of admiration for a much revered friend and artist, rather than a substantial contribution to criticism. The second article is by Frank N. Dauster ("El teatro de Xavier Villaurrutia, *Estaciones,* 1, 1956, pp. 479-487). Dauster comments on the principal themes which Villaurrutia develops in his plays, and establishes a relationship between the dramatic themes and the poetic ones. Dauster calls this article an "ojeada a la obra dramática," and it does not go much beyond that limitation.

As a part of his important work *Imagen de la poesía mexicana contemporánea* (México, Imprenta Universitaria, 1959), Raúl Leiva devotes an entire chapter to Villaurrutia's poetry (pp. 151-163). Leiva reviews previous criticism on Villaurrutia, particularly that of Alí Chumacero and Ramón Xirau, and then comments on the various

---

I took this date to be authoritative, only to find out subsequently that the year 1903 was easily verified in the national archives as being the correct year of birth. See my article "La fecha de nacimiento de Xavier Villaurrutia" (*Revista Iberoamericana,* 33, 1967, pp. 131-132) for further documentation and commentary on the question.

collections of poems with special concentration on *Nostalgia de la muerte*. Leiva is insistently social in his criticism, however, and his judgment of Villaurrutia is consequently somewhat unbalanced. In an article published the same year Luis Leal discussed Villaurrutia's important secondary role as a critic ("Xavier Villaurrutia, crítico," *Estaciones*, 4, 1959, pp. 3-14). Leal is of the opinion that Villaurrutia's major contribution in this area is that of having raised remarkably the general level of Mexican criticism. Immediately following the text of the article Leal presents a selection of Villaurrutia's movie criticism (pp. 15-27).

In 1960, two articles appeared which merit attention. The first, a short article by Giuseppe Bellini ("La poesía de Xavier Villaurrutia," *Letterature moderne*, 10, 1960, pp. 20-27), pursues a relationship between Octavio Paz and his *El laberinto de la soledad* and the theme of solitude as expressed in Villaurrutia's poetry. The second, originally a lecture given in 1957, is by Tomás Segovia ("Xavier Villaurrutia," *Revista Mexicana de Literatura*, oct.-dic. de 1960, pp. 49-63). This is a sensitive and personal appreciation of both life and artistic achievement, in which perhaps the most important assertion is that, though Villaurrutia took much from surrealism, from Heidegger, or from Rilke, he was still supremely and uniquely himself.

1961-1971

Several general studies of the "Contemporáneos" group appeared during this most recent period, each with important material on Villaurrutia. In his *Ensayos sobre poesía mexicana: Asedio a los Contemporáneos* (México, Andrea, 1963), Frank N. Dauster reproduces the article on Villaurrutia's poetry (pp. 17-29) which had appeared earlier in *Estaciones*. My own book, *Los Contemporáneos: 1920-1932* (México, Andrea, 1964), includes commentary and bibliography on Villaurrutia (pp. 83-91, 125-126, 141-144). The unpublished Ph.D. dissertation of Manuel de Ezcurdia, with appropriate attention given to Villaurrutia, was presented at the University of California, Berkeley, in 1964 under the title of "La aparición del grupo Contemporáneos en la poesía y en la crítica mexicanas, 1920-1931."

José Rojas Garcidueñas discusses Villaurrutia's role as critic of literature and art ("Xavier Villaurrutia, crítico," *Nivel*, 25 de enero, 1961), and the British scholar Donald Shaw concerns himself with some universal relationships in Villaurrutia's plays ("Pasión y verdad en el teatro de Villaurrutia," *Revista Iberoamericana,* 28, 1962, pp. 337-346). Huberto Batis writes on three of the fundamental focal points of the *nocturnos* ("Vida-Amor-Muerte en los nocturnos de Xavier Villaurrutia," *Revista Mexicana de Literatura,* marzo-abril, 1964), and César Rodríguez Chicharro has two articles on important aspects of Villaurrutia's style ("Disemia y paronomasia en la poesía de Xavier Villaurrutia," *La Palabra y el Hombre,* abril-junio, 1964, pp. 249-260; "Correlación y paralelismo en la poesía de Xavier Villaurrutia, *Ibid.,* enero-marzo, 1966(pp. 81-90). Sandra M. Cypess' "The Influence of the French Theatre in the Plays of Xavier Villaurrutia" (*Latin American Theatre Review,* Fall 1969, pp. 9-15) is a careful study of contact and tradition, and Eugene L. Moretta studies Villaurrutia's verse in his Ph.D. dissertation ("The Poetic Achievement of Xavier Villaurrutia," Harvard, 1969). Juan García Ponce compares Villaurrutia and Jorge Cuesta in his essay "La noche y la llama" (*Cinco ensayos,* Guanajuato, Universidad de Guanajuato, 1969, pp. 30-62. The most recent major contribution to Villaurrutia criticism is Frank Dauster's excellent book in the Twayne World Author Series: *Xavier Villaurrutia* (New York, Twayne, 1971).

An important editorial and critical achievement is the second and more complete edition of Villaurrutia's works. This volume appeared under the broader title *Obras* (México, FCE, 1966), and represents a substantial enlargement of the 1953 edition. The introductory essay by Alí Chumacero is extended to include comments on Villaurrutia's prose fiction and critical essays, and the bibliographic section of this edition, done by Luis Mario Schneider, is far more complete than the corresponding section in the earlier publication. It includes an extensive primary bibliography, both of items published separately and those published in journals, and an exhaustive gathering of secondary sources. In addition to poetry and drama, the volume includes prose fiction, a reprinting of the critical essays in *Textos y pretextos* (México, Casa de España, 1940), and previously uncollected essays placed under the general title of "Juicios y prejuicios." [11] The immense task of compiling and ordering the texts themselves was done by Alí Chumacero, Luis Mario Schneider, and Miguel Capistrán. The

---

[11] According to members of the family, this title was one which Villaurrutia himself had mentioned prior to his death.

primary weakness of this edition is a lack of indication of sources of previous publication. Even the short commentary on textual sources which was a part of the 1953 edition has been removed, and additional changes have been made with no further explanation.

Critical Method

Previous criticism on Villaurrutia's poetry can be seen from three fundamental perspectives: the biography of the poet and his relationship to his literary period and to other people around him; a particular theme or technique in Villaurrutia's poetic production; expression and development in one or more of the principal collections. I shall attempt to keep each of these views in mind, but the central purpose here will be to order and analyze synthetically without insistence on biography or chronology.

My study moves in general from the specific to the abstract, with a view to careful analysis and ultimate evaluation of the poet's work. [12] Chapter II deals with lexicon and syntax and chapter III with metrical classifications, alliteration, enjambement, and patterns of paronomasia. [13] Chapter IV considers Villaurrutia's use of figurative language in the internal ordering of his poems, examining systems of imagery and certain insistent symbols, such as night, the sea, and the nocturnal street. Chapter V relates the internal systems of Villaurrutia's poetry to outside reality. The themes of love, death, and solitude are the principal reference points in this relationship. Chapter VI is an evaluation of Villaurrutia's poetry in its own terms and as part of a larger literary and cultural whole.

---

[12] I express a considerable debt in the essential foundations of this study to Monroe C. Beardsley's fundamental treatise *Aesthetics: Problems in the Philosophy of Criticism* (New York, Harcourt Brace, 1958).

[13] These chapters depend particularly on careful quantification within the total corpus of material, and a key-word-in-context computer-aided concordance to the poetry of Villaurrutia has been used extensively in isolating and ordering significant patterns.

CHAPTER II

LEXICON AND SYNTAX

General

In 1927 Villaurrutia published in the journal *Ulises* a brief poem which he entitled "Poesía." [1] The first stanza of this composition, which can be seen as a kind of *ars poética*, illuminates a fundamental relationship between the poet and the stuff of poetry:

> Eres la compañía con quien hablo
> de pronto, a solas.
> Te forman las palabras
> que salen del silencio
> y del tanque de sueño en que me ahogo
> libre hasta despertar. [2]

For Villaurrutia the process of poetic creation was essentially verbal, in which words and their multiple relationships produce the reality of poetic form. The "tanque de sueño" image, with its limpid surface and hidden profundity, is suggestive of these same two dimensions in the poet's use of "las palabras" of poetry. Villaurrutia's lexicon is in general relatively simple, with few recondite terms or striking

---

[1] *Ulises*, Núm. 4 (octubre de 1927), p. 3. The poem was published again as a part of *Décima muerte y otros poemas no coleccionados* (México, 1941), with the following comment by the poet: "De haberlo escrito a tiempo, debió figurar al frente de mis *Reflejos*." The editors of the two editions of Villaurrutia's works have followed the somewhat whimsical commentary, and have included this composition as the first in the *Reflejos* collection.

[2] "Poesía," *Obras* (México, FCE, 1966), p. 26. All subsequent poetry citations will be taken from this edition, and will be identified by title and page number at the end of the quotation.

neologisms. Often, however, these lexical elements are arranged in such a way as to produce syntactical, figurative, and conceptual complexities far beyond the apparent simplicity of the language being used.

The short composition "Tranvías," taken from "Suite del insomio" in *Reflejos,* is another example:

Casas que corren locas
de incendio, huyendo
de sí mismas,
entre los esqueletos de las otras
inmóviles, quemadas ya. (p. 42).

The lexical elements of this poem are very simple and there is but one image, that of lighted street cars moving past stationary and unlighted ones. However, the insistent use of run-on lines and the symbolic dimension of such words as "locas," "incendio," "esqueletos," and "quemadas" take us far beyond that simple beginning point. The lines flow into one another, and suggest in their movement both the fevered press of life and the burned shells of death.

"Nocturno solo," from *Nostalgia de la muerte,* as also representative of these two aspects:

Soledad, aburrimiento,
vano silencio profundo,
líquida sombra en que me hundo,
vacío del pensamiento.
Y ni siquiera el acento
de una voz indefinible
que llegue hasta el imposible
rincón de un mar infinito
a iluminar con su grito
este naufragio invisible. (pp. 50-51).

Here again the lexicon is simple, and the poem is arranged in two truncated syntactical elements. Progressive boredom and solitude are represented first as silent liquidity and then as a solitary shipwreck at sea. Prefundity and limitlessness are suggested by "imposible rincón," "mar infinito," "naufragio invisible," as well as by the tentativeness of the present subjunctive verb form "llegue."

A final example of this fundamental relationship is stanza V of "Décima muerte":

No duermo para que al verte
llegar lenta y apagada,
para que al oír pausada
tu voz que silencios vierte,
para que al tocar la nada
que envuelve tu cuerpo yerto,
para que a tu olor desierto
pueda, sin sombra de sueño,
saber que de ti me adueño,
sentir que muero despierto. (p. 71).

Once again the lexicon is limited and simple, but in its careful form and studied antitheses the *décima* is strongly reminiscent of the baroque. The essential contradictions contained in such phrases as "tu voz que silencios vierte," "para que al tocar la nada," "sentir que muero despierto," give the stanza a complexity which is beyond the simplicities of rhyme scheme and lexicon.

Taking this duality as a fundamental relationship, then, several other general considerations need to be mentioned. For example, while the lexicon is relatively simple, it does show considerable variety. Terms asociated with Christianity and Catholicism occur with some frequence, especially in the very early works (ángelus, breviario, rosario, sacramento, etc.), [3] as does the vocabulary of romantic love (amar, besar, cariño, corazón, frenesí, labios, mujer, temblar, etc.). [4] There are some cultural or geographical references (Argos, Boston, New Haven, Noemí, Ulises, etc.), [5] as well as others which reflect the modern technical world (Asensor, camouflage, carretera, grabar, placa, telegrafía, tren, etc.). [6] Physiological and medical terminology is used frequently, especially in reference to parts, processes, and infirmities of the body (anestesiado, arteria, cicatriz, diástole, linfa, nervio, retina, sudor, úlcera, vena, etc.). [7]

---

[3] Alma, ángelus, bíblico, breviario, capilla, devoto, dios, divino, iglesia, Laus Deo, resurrección, rosario, sacramento, señor.

[4] Abrazar, amado, amar, amor, besar, cariño, corazón, dulce, enamorado, febrilmente, frenesí, labios, mano, mujer, ojos, querer, suspirar, temblar.

[5] Alemana, Argos, Boston, North Carolina, Eva, New Haven, Nilo, Noemí, Ulises.

[6] Asensor, azogue, brújula, camouflage, carretera, cigarrillo, corroer, disco, ensamblar, grabar, hospital, hotel, mica, moldura, muselina, obrero, placa, telegrafía, tragaluz, tren, vidrio, yeso.

[7] Aliento, anestesiado, arteria, axila, boca, brazo, cabeza, capilar, cara, carne, cicatriz, circular, congelar, contaminar, corazón, cordón, cuerpo, dedo,

A sensorial dimension in Villaurrutia's use of poetic language is also apparent. Words of visual or chromatic quality are the most numerous, [8] and, though not so frequent, words with a thermic appeal are used often. [9] Terms suggesting touch, [10] smell, [11] and hearing [12] are used less, but still more often than those words having a gustatory quality. [13] Using once more Villaurrutia's "tanque de sueño" image, those words with sensorial overtones appear on the ever-changing surface of the poems, but suggest a profundity which extends beneath that surface. Also, the same duality can be seen in a number of lexical elements which are charged with a kind of subterranean emotion (alucinado, cólera, delirante, embozado, involuntario, presentimiento, sediento, etc.). [14] These terms establish a hallucinated and anguished searching beneath the sensorial representation of the world.

In addition to the deceptively simple lexicon already commented on, Villaurrutia often uses popular or clichéd phrases in unexpected ways. For example, the statue in "Nocturno de la estatua" utters the following words: "estoy muerta de sueño." (p. 47). This phrase is a commonplace which might be rendered in English as "I'm dead tired" or "I'm dead on my feet." However, in the context of the poem the words "muerta" and "sueño" take on complexities which make the phrase the superficial point of reference for a long glance into the conceptual and emotional depths of the poem. Another example is

---

diástole, enfermo, espasmo, esqueleto, fiebre, garganta, labio, latido, lengua, lepra, linfa, llaga, mano, mejilla, morir, muslo, nervio, ojera, ojo, oreja, parálisis, párpado, piel, pie, pulsación, pulso, pupila, respiración, retina, rodilla, salida, sangre, sístole, sudor, úlcera, uña, vena.

[8] Amarillo, amortiguar, azul, blanco, borrar, brillar, cenicienta, color, cristal, diamante, entintar, estatua, iluminado, inmóvil, invisible, lívido, luminoso, luz, mármol, matiz, medusa, mirar, morado, negro, nevado, nocturno, opaco, oro, oscuro, pálido, pecoso, púrpura, reflejo, reluciente, sombra, sombrillo, sonrojar, verde.

[9] Apagar, arder, calor, consumir, enardecido, encender, enfriar, entibiado, fresco, frío, fuego, helado, llama, nevado, nieve.

[10] Blando, contacto, diamante, duro, mármol, palpar.

[11] Aroma, aspirar, emanación, esencia, fragancia, olor, perfume.

[12] Callar, crujir, oír, silencio, silencioso, sonido, sordo.

[13] Amargo, dulce, miel.

[14] Alucinado, angustia, anhelo, ansia, atormentado, avaricia, avidez, celo, cólera, congoja, delirante, descorazonado, desengaño, desnudo, desolado, embozado, escondido, fingir, impuro, involuntario, locura, melancolía, miedo, misterio, oculto, obsesión, olvido, presentimiento, prisionero, rencor, resignado, sediento.

the line "Y comprendo de una vez para nunca" ("Muerte en el frío," p. 67), in which the "nunca" inverts a set phrase so as to reflect the impossibility of understanding rather than its easy accessibility.

Noun

Nominal forms in the poetry of Villaurrutia are those elements which are perhaps the most objective and those least affected by subtle shadings of emotional tone. However, a close examination of frequency and usage reveals that the abstract, the corporeal, the emotional, the temporal, and the sensorial are reflected at times in the substantives which are chosen for frequent use by Villaurrutia.

There are 92 nouns which occur five times or more,[15] of which approximately 30% are used twenty times or more. Several high-frequency nouns are particularly rich in meanings, and bear further consideration.

Sombra (55 occurrences)

The noun *sombra* appears in multiple contexts. It often stands unmodified in a kind of primary chromatic sense ("Y no basta cerrar los ojos en la sombra", "Nocturno miedo," p. 45). Independent personalized existence is expressed ("hasta que la *sombra* se asombra", "Nocturno eterno," p. 51), and the word suggests human form ("y busco mi *sombra* en vano.", "Nocturno grito," p. 46) and human emotion which is hidden and unexpressed ("ni la *sombra* inconfesa de un desear.", "Con la mirada humilde," p. 6). *Sombra* has liquidity ("líquida *sombra* en que me hundo,", "Nocturno solo," p. 50) and even at times the circulation and congealing of blood is implied ("sa-

---

[15] Reduced to singular form and in descending order of frequency, these nouns are: 55: sombra; 53: sueño; 51: ojo; 49: silencio; 48: noche; 45: rosa; 44: vida; 42: voz; 40: mano; 39: muerte; 38: cuerpo; 37: agua; 34: cielo, corazón; 32: vez; 30: luz, miedo, palabra; 28: boca; 27: mar; 25: amor; 24: labio; 21: aire, sangre; 20: espejo, tarde; 18: fin, mirada, nieve; 17: día, sed; 16: angustia, primavera, soledad; 15: esperanza, grito, nube, piel, viento; 14: calle, hombre, instante; 13: deseo, tierra; 12: paso, secreto; 11: alcoba, alma, ansia, brazos, dedos, hojas, nombre, puerta, sol; 10: cara, dos, echo, luna, techo, ventana; 9: color, estrella, herida, momento, mujer, North Carolina, paisaje; 8: calor, ceniza, cristal, estatua, forma, humo, lluvia, oreja, sabor; 7: cosa, goce, pensamiento, pie, sonrisa; 6: Dios, red, rincón, Señor; 5: dueño, lecho, perfume, poeta, tren.

carla de la sangre de su *sombra*,", "Nocturno de la estatua," p. 47). At times laborious working beneath the surface can be seen ("panal de *sombra* encarnada,", "Soneto de la granada," p. 78), as well as the shadowy remains of something usually more substantial ("nada son sino *sombras* de palabras", "Nocturno eterno," p. 52).

Sueño (53 occurrences)

Villaurrutia uses this noun almost without exception in its meaning of "dream" and not "sleep." With that meaning, the dream fantasy is profound and all encompassing ("de un *sueño* cada vez más profundo y más largo.", "Estancias nocturnas," p. 63), something mysterious ("pecado ajeno y *sueño* misterioso,", "Nocturno mar," p. 60) and at the same time empty and cold ("de un *sueño* hueco y frío en el que ya no queda", "Nocturno," p. 53).

Noche (48 occurrences)

The word occurs occasionally, especially in the earlier poems, with a generalized temporal meaning ("una *noche* de luna,", "Le pregunté al poeta," p. 4). More frequently the night is personified ("La *noche* surge envuelta en su manto de polvo.", "Cuando la tarde . . . ," p. 62) or is perceived as a powerful presence whose effect is felt in many ways ("¡Al fin llegó la *noche* a inundar mis oídos", "Nocturno," p. 54). The night brings with it a sense of darkness and emptiness in which the sounds and the objects of the day take on rather different qualities ("En la *noche* resuena, como en un mundo hueco, / el ruido de mis pasos prolongados, distantes.", "Estancias nocturnas," p. 62).

Voz (42 occurrences)

This noun has, particularly in the earlier poems, a conventional meaning ("Ya percibí tu *voz*,", "Presentimiento," p. 9). Often, however, the voice is disembodied ("sin más que una mirada y una *voz*", "Nocturno en que nada se oye," p. 47) or is one of the concrete indications of life in a shadowy nocturnal world ("alzar la *voz* y preguntar 'quién vive' ", "Nocturno eterno," p. 51). This noun also functions as the base element in one of Villaurrutia's fragment puns ("cae mi *voz* / y mi *voz* que madura / y mi *voz* quemadura", "Nocturno en que nada se oye," p. 47).

Muerte (39 occurrences)

This noun is hardly used in a general depersonalized sense, but rather with an individualized meaning. Death is often personified ("En vano amenazas, *Muerte*,", "Décima muerte," X, p. 73), or is seen as something entirely personal and individual ("mi *muerte* que no puedo compartir ni llorar,", "Muerte en el frío," p. 67). For the poet, death is to be labored over and perfected ("donde se nutre y perfecciona la *muerte*.", "Muerte en el frío," p. 67), and is even suggestive of the moment of orgasm in sexual experience ("provocando el segundo de *muerte*", "Noche," p. 28). However, his fear of death knows no bounds ("ese miedo mortal a la *muerte*,", "Paradoja del miedo," p. 69).

Verb

The frequency patterns of the verb are rather different than those for the noun. For exemple, there are only 71 verbs which occur five times or more [16] and of those only about 10% appear with a frequency of thirty times or more. On the other hand, some common verbs appear far more frequently than any of the nouns catalogued (for example, *ser* appears 224 times and *haber* 73 times). Also, there is a rather high density of verbal constructions. Verbs occur a total of 1557 times in Villaurrutia's poems and appear in all the conventional tenses and moods. [17] Within this total figure some forms show a high frequency. For example, the present indicative tense appears in 53% of the total verbal occurrences, as compared to approximately 5% each for the preterit indicative and imperfect indicative. The infinitive is

---

[16] 224: ser; 73: haber; 49: saber; 47: querer; 45: dejar; 40: estar; 38: decir; 29: ir; 28: mirar; 27: amar, dar, oír, sentir; 26: llegar; 21: morir, ver; 20: hacer; 19: caer; 18: cerrar; 17: encontrar; 16: llorar, salir, vivir, mover; 15: pensar, tener; 14: despertar, poner; 13: esperar; 12: seguir; 11: buscar, subir; 10: jugar, llevar; 9: hallar, hundir, huir; 8: acariciar, callar, hablar, inclinar; 7: abrir, atrever, caminar, guardar, respirar, temblar; 6: ahogar, alcanzar, dormir, encender, herir, mandar, latir, pasar, tender, tomar; 5: arder, besar, borrar, brillar, comprender, correr, crecer, empezar, existir, perseguir, preguntar, saciar, surgir, tocar.

[17] Observable patterns, in descending order of frequency, are as follows: 808: present indicative; 339: infinitive; 79: preterit indicative; 70: imperfect indicative; 51: future indicative; 51: gerundive; 45: present subjunctive; 22: imperative forms; 19: imperfect subjunctive; 15: conditional indicative. Perfective forms (excluding *hay*) total 58, as follows: 50: present perfect; 2: future perfect; 2: conditional perfect; 2: present perfect subjunctive; 1: pluperfect.

the second most frequent form, occurring in approximately 22% of the total number, and the future indicative and the present subjunctive have a frequency of 3% and 2%, respectively. The gerundive form appears as 3% of the total, and the conditional indicative and imperfect subjunctive only 1% each.

Several general observations may be made on the basis of these visible patterns in the use of the verb in Villaurrutia's poetry. First, as was the case also with the noun, Villaurrutia uses common verbs of very high frequency in the language and represents with them concepts or actions on a multiplicity of levels. The verb *ser,* for example, goes far beyond the conventional meaning in its association with the many reverberations of the metaphysical problem of being and nonbeing. Second, the frequent use of the present indicative tense, the infinitive, and the less frequent use of the gerundive form underline a curious nonspecificity in Villaurrutia's poetry in which time and place are blurred in favor of the sharp internalized anguish of an actual or potential moment. A few examples will illustrate these comments.

The present indicative communicates a sensorial and often anguished immediacy:

> El aire juega a las distancias:
> acerca el horizonte,
> echa a volar los árboles
> y levanta vidrieras entre los ojos y el paisaje.
> ("Aire," p. 29)

> o cuando de una boca que no existe
> sale un grito inaudito
> que nos echa a la cara su luz viva
> y se apaga y nos deja una ciega sordera
> ("Nocturno eterno," p. 51).

The infinitive is often used in conjunction with the present indicative to extend this sense of nonspecificity. The infinitive is seldom nominalized, but does appear at times in the *al* + infinitive construction as an expression of temporality ("El reloj se detiene *al dar* la hora,", "Yo no quiero ... ," p. 8; "Para que *al tocar* la nada," "Décima muerte," V, p. 71). However, the most common structure using the infinitive is a kind of open form in which person and time are not marked:

Soñar, soñar la noche, la calle, la escalera
y el grito de la estatua desdoblando la esquina.

Correr hacia la estatua y encontrar sólo el grito,
querer tocar el grito y sólo hallar el eco,
querer asir el eco y encontrar sólo el muro
y correr hacia el muro y tocar un espejo.
Hallar en el espejo la estatua asesinada,
sacarla de la sangre de su sombra,
vestirla en un cerrar de ojos,
acariciarla como a una hermana imprevista
y jugar con las fichas de sus dedos
y contar a su oreja cien veces cien cien veces
hasta oírla decir: "estoy muerta de sueño."

("Nocturno de la estatua," pp. 46-47).

There are 21 verbal elements in this poem, of which only two are
not infinitives ("desdoblando," line 2; "estoy," line 13). One infinitive
form is nominalized ("un cerrar de ojos," line 9), and the remaining
eighteen forms underscore strongly in their nonconjugation the shadowy, nontemporal search which is evident in the poem.

The gerund is another verbal form which often expresses this same
sense of extended present. The *ir* + gerund construction appears at
times ("la soledad *se va ahondando*,", "Décimas de nuestro amor,"
IV, p. 80; "y ya siente un amor que *va enjugando*,", "Él," p. 22),
but the most frequent construction is that in which the gerund appears
without any auxiliary construction, often in connection with present
indicative and infinitive forms: "Oigo mi corazón *latir sangrando* /
y siempre y nunca igual." ("Inventar la verdad," p. 83).

The other tenses and moods, often in a variety of persons, appear
less frequently but at times quite significantly against this background
of nontemporality and nonindividuality. For example, in "Nocturno
sueño" the past tenses form the principal verbal patterning:

Abría las salas
profundas el sueño
y voces delgadas
corrientes de aire
entraban

Del barco del cielo
del papel pautado
caía la escala

por donde mi cuerpo
bajaba

El cielo en el suelo
como en un espejo
la calle azogada
dobló mis palabras

Me robó mi sombra
la sombra cerrada
Quieto de silencio
oí que mis pasos
pasaban

El frío de acero
a mi mano ciega
armó con su daga
Para darme muerte
la muerte esperaba

Y al doblar la esquina
un segundo largo
mi mano acerada
encontró mi espalda

Sin gota de sangre
sin ruido ni peso
a mis pies clavados
vino a dar mi cuerpo

Lo tomé en los brazos
lo llevé a mi lecho

Cerraba las alas
profundas el sueño (pp. 48-49).

There are seventeen verbal elements in this poem, of which only two
are not imperfect or preterit indicative (the verbs *dar* and *doblar* in
lines 24 and 26). The complete absence of the present indicative is
worthy of note, and the interplay between preterit and imperfect
creates an unusual shading of past time. Also, the more specific sub-
jects for the past tense forms, particularly those in the preterit, represent a contrast with the frequent nonspecificity of the present tense
used in other compositions.

The shadings of potentiality inherent in the future and conditional
tenses are often used to advantage by the poet, as are the nonspecific

or contrary-to-fact dimensions available in the tenses of the subjunctive mood. These qualities are exemplified well in these lines from "Nocturno de los ángeles":

> Se diría que las calles fluyen dulcemente en la noche.
> Las luces no son tan vivas que logren desvelar el secreto,
> el secreto que los hombres que van y vienen conocen,
> porque todos están en el secreto
> y nada se ganaría con partirlo en mil pedazos
> si, por el contrario, es tan dulce guardarlo
> y compartirlo sólo con la persona elegida.
>
> Si cada uno dijera en un momento dado,
> en sólo una palabra, lo que piensa,
> las cinco letras del DESEO formarían una enorme
> > cicatriz luminosa.... (p. 55).

At times the verbal patterning is rich and complex, as can be seen in the text of "Nocturno grito":

> Tengo miedo de mi voz
> y busco mi sombra en vano.
>
> ¿Será mía aquella sombra
> sin cuerpo que va pasando?
> ¿Y mía la voz perdida
> que va la calle incendiando?
>
> ¿Qué voz, qué sombra, qué sueño
> despierto que no he soñado
> serán la voz y la sombra
> y el sueño que me han robado?
>
> Para oír brotar la sangre
> de mi corazón cerrado,
> ¿pondré la oreja en mi pecho
> como en el pulso la mano?
>
> Mi pecho estará vacío
> y yo descorazonado
> y serán mis manos duros
> pulso de mármol helado. (p. 46).

There are twelve verbal forms used in the poem: future (5); present indicative (2); present perfect (2); gerundive (2); infinitive (1). The present tense appears twice in the first two lines and serves as a backdrop for the multiple shadings of the other patterns. The future tense appears in each of the following stanzas with the strong representation of future of possibility, and in all except the last stanza it is used in an interrogative sentence. A dimension of uncertainty is thus established against the present indicative statements of the first stanza, and the gerundive constructions of the second stanza tend to sustain this double perception. The perfective forms in the third stanza provide a preterit dimension while at the same time maintaining a strong connection to the present. The two future verbs of the final stanza, which appear in a non-interrogatory context, can be taken as both declarative and future of probability, and thus provide one more aspect in the complex verbal patterning of the poem.

Adjective

Contrary to what might be expected, the frequency of adjectival patterns in the poetry of Villaurrutia is much lower than that of the noun or the verb. There are 49 adjectives which have a frequency of five or more, [18] of which only 25% have a frequency of fifteen or more. The possessives are the only high frequency forms, with *mi* (247), *su* (199), *tú* (137), and *nuestro* (35) as the four most used adjectival patterns. Those forms which might easily represent the kind of multiple shadings one would see as consistent with Villaurrutia's poetry have a much lower frequency. *Duro*, for example, occurs nineteen times, with such adjectives as *oscuro* (15), *muerto* (14), *nocturno* (10), and *helado* (6) appearing even less.

Such reduced frequency, however, does not diminish the relative complexity of adjectival patterning as compared to that of the noun or the verb.

The most frequent adjectival usage is that of a single adjective, either in pre- or post-position, modifying a single noun. As is normal in the language, the pre-positioned adjectives tend to define and those

---

[18] These forms, reduced to masculine singular, are as follows: 247: mi; 199: su; 137: tú; 35: nuestro; 33: este; 32: otro; 21: mío; 19: duro; 17: despierto; 15: aquel, oscuro, profundo; 14: inmóvil, ese, muerto; 13: desnudo, secreto; 12: dormido, mudo, silencioso; 11: largo; 10: eterno, nocturno, olvidado, perdido; 9: inútil, lejano, rojo, viejo; 8: invisible; 7: cerrado, nuevo, pálido, último, verde; 6: abierto, ajeno, alto, helado, húmedo, imprevisto; 5: cercano, desierto, gris, interminable, pobre, trémulo.

in post-position to compare or contrast. The following lines are examples:

> el vulnerable talón (p. 88)
> y amarillo el tapiz (p. 12)
> en el profundo cuerpo de la noche, (p. 55)
> y en tu blando mirar halló deleite; (p. 23)
> de una palabra antigua (p. 52)
> busquen mi piel dormida y mi boca despierta. (p. 84)
> un humo delgado (p. 40)
> en que un cielo alucinante (p. 72).

A prepositional phrase often modifies a single noun, which again is a common pattern in the language: "los barcos *de cartón*" (p. 40); "la rosa *de ceniza*," (p. 58); "porque en el plato *de porcelana*" (p. 30). At times this construction produces some very unusual effects, as for example in these lines from "Cézanne":

> Junto a las naranjas de abiertos poros
> las manzanas se pintan demasiado,
> y a los duraznos, por su piel de quince años,
> dan deseos de acariciarlos. (p. 31).

In their function as adjectival elements, the prepositional phrases in lines 1 and 3 of the strophe enhance the essentially pictorial comparisons of the poem.

At times Villaurrutia blurs the traditional limits between a single noun and a single modifying adjective, often with the effect of producing vagueness and secondary or even tertiary levels of meaning. Perhaps the best example of this blurring is to be found in "Nocturno rosa," in which the noun *rosa* is used with a number of modifying adjectives. In many of these occurrences there is no ambiguity in the adjectival-nominal relationship. Lines such as "Pero mi rosa no es la rosa fría" (p. 57) or "ni la rosa encerada," (p. 57) raise no questions about the limitations of noun and adjective. However, many times in the poem these traditional relationships are confused, as can be seen in the following stanza:

> No es la rosa veleta,
> ni la úlcera secreta,
> ni la rosa puntual que da la hora,
> ni la brújula rosa marinera. (p. 57).

The "rosa veleta" of the first line of the stanza can be seen in at least two ways. It could be the noun *rosa* modified by a second nominal element which takes the function here of adjective, or it could be "veleta", as noun form being modified by a chromatic or formal adjective "rosa". The final line, which represents the flower-like shape of a mariner's compass, is even more complex. Here the noun "rosa" is modified by two elements, one a post-positioned adjective and the other a noun, both of which have a relationship which is interrupted by the embedded noun form *rosa*. The final image is a striking one, but one in which the traditional nominal-adjective construction is altered.

In addition to the patterns involving essentially one nominal and one adjectival form, Villaurrutia very often uses multiples of both nouns and adjectives. For example, at times a noun will have both a pre-positioned and a post-positioned adjective, a construction which utilizes the positioning of the forms as well as the differences in meaning between the two:

> con una silenciosa marea inesperada (p. 54)
> con azules agujas ensartadas (p. 60)
> y tus involuntarios movimientos oscuros (p. 61).

Another common multiple pattern is that of two pre-positioned or post-positioned adjectives modifying a single substantive form:

> Al sol, borrosa y lejana, (p. 42)
> una constelación más antigua, más viva aún que las otras. (p. 55)
> tu carne dura y frutada. (p. 30)
> de un tacto sutil y blando, (p. 71)
> Ella toda se ha vuelto más devota y más triste (p. 11)
> como un poco de aire cálido e invisible
> mezclado al aire duro y frío que respiras; (p. 54)
> La tierra hecha impalpable silencioso silencio, (p. 52)
> reminiscente y roja rosa. (p. 17)
> una sutil y lúcida avaricia. (p. 77).

The function of this doubled adjectival construction is varied. At times, it serves to accentuate a single quality by repeating the same form ("El mar que hace un trabajo lento y lento", p. 59) or by using two adjectival forms which are easily related ("el ruido de mis pasos prolongados, distantes.", p. 62). At times, however, the adjectival forms are less comparable and often require a less obvious relation ("una suspensa y luminosa duda;", p. 76; "la impensable callada nieve negra.", p. 63).

A natural extension of the doubling of adjectival elements modifying a single noun are those constructions in which three or even four adjectives stand in relation to a single substantive form:

> Al fin llegó la noche a despertar palabras
> ajenas, desusadas, propias, desvanecidas: (p. 53)
> Su boca está muy pálida, entreabierta, doliente, (p. 11)
> a convertir mi envoltura
> opaca, febril, cambiante, (p. 71)
> Es cóncava y oscura y tibia y silenciosa, (p. 60)
> con la vida secreta, muda e imperceptible (p. 68).

Here the constructions always occur in post-position, and offer many more shadings of meaning because of the variety of adjectives included. The reinforcing of the doubled adjective is somewhat reduced, and the impression is generally that of a piling up of differing qualities or sense impressions ("Después un ruido sordo, azul y numeroso,", p. 52).

There are also a number of constructions in which a single adjective modifies more than one noun:

> olvidos olvidados y deseos, (p. 59)
> perfiles y perfumes mutilados, (p. 60)
> de corales arterias y raíces
> y venas y medusas capilares. (p. 60).

These constructions are relatively infrequent, but offer an interesting contrast to the adjectival doubling already commented on. Here the adjective is the stable element in the phrase, and the complexity is found in the extension of the noun forms.

There are a number of constructions in which a kind of doubling appears again, but here by combining two sets of single noun — adjective constructions. The most common form here is noun — adjective + noun — adjective, but at times the variation adjective — noun + noun — adjective also appears:

> el reflejo olvidado y el ruido interrumpido, (p. 62)
> la soledad opaca y la sombra ceniza (p. 52)
> memorias angustiosas, temores congelados, (p. 53)

es tu palabra trunca, tus gemidos ajenos (p. 61)
húmedas ramas y nubes delgadas. (p. 27).

Occasionally the lines of demarcation between one pattern and another are blurred, as can be seen in this line in which adjectival complexity is increased by a possibility of at least two readings: "Ni tu silencio duro cristal de dura roca," (p. 59). By seeing a possible point of juncture either before or after "duro", it is possible to make that element either a post-positioned adjective modifying "silencio" or a pre-positioned adjective, modifying "cristal", as a part of an adjective — noun + adjective — noun construction. Another example of the same pattern is the following line: "noche larga y cruel noche que ya no es noche" (p. 50).

Other Patterns

In a recent article César Rodríguez Chicharro finds rigorously mathematical systems of correlation and parallelism in Villaurrutia's poetry, [19] and designates them as baroque artifices which Villaurrutia used consciously "por obtener ritmos harmoniosos, por alcanzar determinados refinamientos estilísticos" (p. 90). Rodríguez Chicharro's study distinguishes clearly these two patterns, and gives abundant examples of each, often with corresponding diagramatic formulae which make more apparent the complexities of verbal design. However, he does not consider several others which are just as evident, and which should be considered here.

As has already been suggested, Villaurrutia's poetry, particularly during the *Nostalgia de la muerte* period, has a shadowy and subterranean quality which is often enhanced by syntactical and typographical devices. At times, for example, punctuation is drastically reduced or at times even entirely eliminated, and rhetorical patterns are used to give a kind of repetitive sense of direction to an otherwise meandering composition. The most common pattern of this sort is the use of anaphora, which appears in a number of poems. [20]

---

[19] "Correlación y paralelismo en la poesía de Xavier Villaurrutia," *La palabra y el hombre* (enero-marzo de 1966), 81-90.

[20] The most notable examples are to be found in the following: "Nocturno," pp. 44-45; "Nocturno," pp. 53-54; "Nocturno de los ángeles," pp. 55-57; "Nocturno rosa," pp. 57-58; "Nocturno de la alcoba," pp. 60-61; "Cuando la tarde . . . ," pp. 61-62; "Muerte en el frío," pp. 66-68; "Vol-

An examination of the text of "Nocturno eterno," which comes from the collection *Nostalgia de la muerte,* will illustrate:

Cuando los hombres alzan los hombros y pasan
o cuando dejan caer sus nombres
hasta que la sombra se asombra
cuando un polvo más fino aún que el humo
5   se adhiere a los cristales de la voz
y a la piel de los rostros y las cosas

cuando los ojos cierran sus ventanas
al rayo del sol pródigo y prefieren
la ceguera al perdón y el silencio al sollozo

10   cuando la vida o lo que así llamamos inútilmente
y que no llega sino con un nombre innombrable
se desnuda para saltar al lecho
y ahogarse en el alcohol o quemarse en la nieve

cuando la vi cuando la vid cuando la vida
15   quiere entregarse cobardemente y a oscuras
sin decirnos siquiera el precio de su nombre

cuando en la soledad de un cielo muerto
brillan unas estrellas olvidadas
y es tan grande el silencio del silencio
20   que de pronto quisiéramos que hablara

o cuando de una boca que no existe
sale un grito inaudito
que nos echa a la cara su luz viva
y se apaga y nos deja una ciega sordera

25   o cuando todo ha muerto
tan dura y lentamente que da miedo
alzar la voz y preguntar "quién vive"

dudo si responder
a la muda pregunta con un grito
30   por temor de saber que ya no existe

porque acaso la voz tampoco vive
sino como un recuerdo en la garganta

---

ver . . . ," pp. 69-70; "Amor condusse noi ad una morte," pp. 76-77; "Nuestro amor," pp. 82-83; "Deseo," pp. 84-85.

y no es la noche sino la ceguera
lo que llena de sombra nuestros ojos

35 y porque acaso el grito es la presencia
de una palabra antigua
opaca y muda que de pronto grita

porque vida silencio piel y boca
y soledad recuerdo cielo y humo
40 nada son sino sombras de palabras
que nos salen al paso de la noche. (pp. 51-52).

It can be observed that there is almost no punctuation in the entire poem, except for the first capitalized letter in line 1 and the quotation marks in line 27. Against the unstopped flow of the poem, then, there are two visible anaphoric patterns which give some means of control. The first is the repeated use through the first eight strophes of constructions utilizing the adverb of time "cuando". The initial line in each strophe repeats "cuando" and links its temporality to different nouns and verbs. This pattern produces on the one hand a sense of organization in chaos, and on the other a strong perception of related circles or meanderings which turn constantly in on themselves. The sense of multiple concentricity is enhanced by some of the repetitions of the temporal adverb within strophes. For example the immediate repetition in line 2 of "o cuando" gives an immediate sense of gyration. In stanza 5 the pattern is even more complex. The three repetitions of temporality followed by a progressive revelation of the accompanying noun ("cuando la vi cuando la vid cuando la vida", line 14) creates an even greater repetitive sensation.

Stanza 9 is a point of change in the poem and is the only stanza which is not tied to the patterns of anaphora. Stanzas 10-12 change the anaphoric system from that of an adverb of time to a conjunction of causality. The first lines of the final three stanzas use "porque" as the basis of patterning, which serves as a point of connection both to the first person verb of stanza 9 and the series of temporal adverbs of stanzas 1-8. The pattern then becomes the following: anaphora in a repeated adverb of temporality (repeated eleven times in the first eight stanzas), which in turn is connected to the nonrepetitive present tense statement of stanza 10. These two elements are then linked to the anaphora in a conjunction of causality (repeated in the initial line of the last three stanzas).

A related rhetorical figure, which often appears with the same connective function, is that of polysyndeton. For example, in the following lines the conjunction "y" serves to relate and string out some of the disparate elements of the poem:

> Paisaje inmóvil de cuatro colores,
> de cuatro limpios colores:
> azul, lavado azul de las montañas
> y del cielo,
> verde, húmedo verde en el prado
> y en las colinas,
> y gris en la nube compacta,
> y amarillo.
>
> ("Incolor," p. 39);

> Y es el ruido de hojas calcinadas
> que hacen tus pies desnudos al hundirse en la alfombra.
>
> Y es el sudor que moja nuestros muslos
> que se abrazan y luchan y que, luego, se rinden.
>
> Y es la frase que dejas caer, interrumpida.
> Y la pregunta mía que no oyes,
> que no comprendes o que no respondes.
>
> ("Nocturno de la alcoba," p. 61).

CHAPTER III

SOUND AND FORM

If one considers Villaurrutia's poetry from the point of view of
what Monroe Beardsley has called "the sound of the work," [1] certain
basic distinctions become quickly discernible. First, Villaurrutia's
poetry makes use of patterns which are both conventional and non-
conventional. Line lengths, stanza forms, rhyme, and rhythm show
the poet's familiarity with traditional Spanish versification and at the
same time his characteristic use of the non-traditional. Second, this
contrast can be seen largely in chronological terms. Conventional metrical patterning is much more common in *Primeros poemas* and the
last collection, *Canto a la primavera*; the non-conventional patterns are
more frequent in the two intermediate collections, *Reflejos* and *Nostalgia de la muerte*. Third, insistent alliteration and word-plays form
an important aspect of Villaurrutia's poetic expression, particularly
in *Reflejos* and *Nostalgia de la muerte*.

Conventional Forms

Villaurrutia differs sharply from some contemporary poets in his
use of traditional metrics. For example, in contrast to Neruda or
Huidobro, who after their earliest poems rejected almost completely
the notion of traditional metrics, Villaurrutia uses throughout his
works conventional meters, stanza forms, and rhyme schemes.

The most common stanzaic pattern is the quatrain. Twenty-six
compositions, either totally or in large part, use this form as a standard. All but two of the poems come from either *Primeros poemas*

---

[1] *Aesthetics* (New York, Harcourt Brace, 1958), p. 452.

(a total of 17) and *Canto a la primavera* (a total of 7). The following
stanzas are examples:

> Yo no quiero llegar pronto ni tarde,
> me dicta su tic-tac el reloj viejo,
> y al par que inclina su candor la tarde
> se amortiguan las aguas del espejo.
>
> ("Yo no quiero...," p. 8)

> En el agua dormida mi caricia más leve
> se tiende como el perro humilde de la granja;
> la soledad en un impalpable oro llueve,
> y se aclara el ambiente oloroso a naranja.
>
> ("En el agua dormida," p. 21)

> Entonces, con el paso de un dormido despierto,
> sin rumbo y sin objeto nos echamos a andar.
> La noche vierte sobre nosotros su misterio,
> y algo nos dice que morir es despertar.
>
> ("Nocturno miedo," p. 45)

> Dichoso amor el nuestro, que nada y nadie nombra:
> prisionero olvidado, sin luz y sin testigo.
> Amor secreto que convierte en miel la sombra,
> como la florescencia en la cárcel del higo.
>
> ("Madrigal sombrío," p. 84).

In general the compositions in quatrains are also rather conventional in meter and rhyme. Nine poems use an Alexandrine line, six
an hendecasyllabic, and there are scattered examples of other conventional lines. Also, most of the quatrain stanzas have visible consonantal rhyme schemes.

Some poems using a basic quatrain stanza and conventional meter,
however, show variations, as if the poet felt a need to break somewhat any pattern which he establishes. The poem "Tarde," which
is from *Primeros poemas,* is a good example:

> Un maduro perfume de membrillo en las ropas
> blancas y almidonadas... ¡Oh campestre saludo
> del ropero asombrado, que nos abre sus puertas
> sin espejos, enormes y de un tallado rudo!...

> Llena el olor la alcoba, mientras el sol afuera
> camina poco a poco, se duplica en la noria,

bruñe cada racimo, cada pecosa pera,
y le graznan los patos su rima obligatoria.

En todo se deslíe el perfume a membrillo
que salió de la alcoba ... Es como una oración
que supimos de niños ... Si — como el corderillo
prófugo del redil — huyó de la memoria,
hoy, que a nosotros vuelve, se ensancha el corazón.

Dulzura hay en el alma, y juventud, y vida,
y perfume en la tarde que, ya desvanecida,
se va tornando rosa, dejando la fragancia
de la ropa que vela, mientras muere la estancia ... (p. 16).

The poem is in quatrains with Alexandrine lines which rhyme
ABAB. The poet breaks this pattern in several ways, however. For
example, the third stanza has five lines, the fourth of which does not
fit into the stanza rhyme scheme but rather is related to one of the
rhyming elements of the previous stanza. Also, the first and fourth
stanzas show variation in rhyme scheme. Finally, an insistent series
of run-on lines throughout the poem changes significantly the seeming
conventionality of the fourteen-syllable meter with its normal caesura
at mid-point. For example, the first three lines of the first stanza of
the poem show marked *enjambement* with the succeeding lines, and
there is at least one run-on line pattern in each of the succeeding
stanzas. None of these various patterns is sufficient to break the fundamental metrical unity of the poem, but at the same time a sense of
dissatisfaction with established conventional form is evident.

The next most frequent metrical pattern is that of the *décima*.
This stanza is used in two of Villaurrutia's best-known later compositions, "Décima muerte" and "Décimas de nuestro amor," and also
in separate shorter compositions. If one considers separately the numbered sub-divisions of the longer poems, the *décima* is used a total
of twenty-two times in Villaurrutia's poetry.

With very few exceptions, Villaurrutia's *décimas* follow the classical pattern. There is no variation in the octasyllabic line and the
normal rhyme pattern is abbaaccddc. In three cases this pattern varies
slightly. In stanzas V and VI of "Décima muerte," the rhyme scheme
of the final six lines is bccddc and acdccd. Stanza X of "Décimas de
nuestro amor" shows a similar variation in the same lines: accdcd.
These are only slight variations from the norm, and serve primarily

to indicate again Villaurrutia's less than complete subjection to an established classical pattern.

In looking at the metrical and grammatical structure of Villaurrutia's *décimas*, several groupings become apparent. In all but three, the ten lines of the stanza are constructed around a beginning four-line statement followed by different varying patterns of the remaining six lines. Thus, it is possible to see a 4-3-3 pattern or a 4-6 pattern, a 4-2-4, a 4-4-2, or even 4-5-1. An example of the frequent 4-3-3 variation (seven occurrences) is the composition "Nocturno preso," which is as follows:

> Prisionero de mi frente
> el sueño quiere escapar
> y fuera de mí probar
> a todos que es inocente.
> Oigo su voz impaciente,
> miro su gesto y su estado
> amenazador, airado.
> No sabe que soy el sueño
> de otro: si fuera su dueño
> ya lo habría libertado. (p. 49).

The *décima* is visibly separated into three elements. The first of these is the four-line statement, rhyming abba, which comes to an end with a full stop. The following three lines, rhyming acc and with a partial stop after line 5, take the idea and movement of the poem a little further but again are stopped completely with a period. The final three lines, rhyming ddc, resolve the problem of the *décima* and bring the whole construction to a close with the final full stop. The only other metrical complication is the series of two run-on lines in lines 6 through 9.

Equally as frequent (seven occurrences), however, is a 4-6 pattern which utilizes the same introductory period of the first four lines, but is followed by an unstopped series of the remaining six lines. An example of this pattern is stanza IX from "Décimas de nuestro amor":

> Si nada espero, pues nada
> tembló en ti cuando me viste
> y ante mis ojos pusiste
> la verdad más desolada;
> si no brilló en tu mirada
> un destello de emoción,

la sola oscura razón,
la fuerza que a ti me lanza,
perdida toda esperanza,
es... ¡la desesperación! (p. 81)

Here the initial statement is stopped at the end of line 4 by a semicolon, and the following six lines, in spite of the various partial stops
indicated by commas at the end of various lines, are not really separated from each other in any way. The reading must go from line 5
through line 10, with only very brief suspensions in preparation for
the final statement of the stanza.

A third and somewhat less frequent pattern (four occurrences)
uses the same four-line introductory element followed by a 2-4 arrangement of the remaining six lines. The ninth stanza from "Décima
muerte" is exemplary:

Si te llevo en mí prendida
y te acaricio y escondo;
si te alimento en el fondo
de mi más secreta herida;
si mi muerte te da vida
y goce mi frenesí,
¿qué será, Muerte, de ti
cuando al salir yo del mundo,
deshecho el nudo profundo,
tengas que salir de mí? (p. 73).

The first four lines are stopped by a semicolon and represent the
basic point of the composition. The remaining lines show a clear separation, marked with a comma after line 6. The remaining four lines,
set off by question marks, flow together as one unit in spite of the
commas ending several of the lines.

Stanza III from "Décimas de nuestro amor" is unique in its
arrangement. The four-line statement is the same as the other décimas already considered, and is followed by a five-line segment stopped
by a colon in order to set completely apart the strong statement of
the final line:

Pero está mudo e inerme
tu corazón, de tal suerte
que si no me dejas verte
es por no ver en la mía

la imagen de tu agonía:
porque mi muerte es tu muerte. (p. 79).

The effect of the 4-5-1 pattern here is to make even more apparent the movement of the *décima* toward the final line, which is one of the most poignant in Villaurrutia's poems.

There are two exceptions to the basic pattern of the four-line introductory statement. Stanza IV of "Décimas de nuestro amor" has what must be characterized as a 5-5 structural pattern, balanced within itself and yet different and also out of keeping with the other *décima* stanzas. Stanza VIII of the same collection has a 3-3-4 progression, which in a way is a reversal of several of the other patterns already noted. Again, these few variations can be seen as Villaurrutia's characteristic reluctance to accept without change even a form as successful as the *décima*.

Another classical form used repeatedly by Villaurrutia is the sonnet, which appears a total of nine times and in all collections except for *Reflejos*. Again, the basic pattern is one of regularity. Six of Villaurrutia's sonnets have the standard hendecasyllabic meter, with consonantal rhyme in expected patterns: the quatrains rhyming ABBA and with several variants in the tercets (three have the form CDCDCD; two the form CCDEED; a third the more unusual CCDAAC). There are three sonnets, however, which vary somewhat more from the classical pattern, and need further comment.

"Soneto de la granada," which comes from *Canto a la primavera*, has octasyllabic meter but in other respects is regular. The consonantal rhyme scheme in the quatrains is the traditional abba, and the tercets rhyme cdcede. "Ni la leve zozobra," which appears in *Primeros poemas*, is somewhat more free. The meter is Alexandrine, and proper scansion often depends on an *aguda* word at the end of the hemistich. Also, the consonantal rhyme scheme differs from the patterns already discussed: the quatrains rhyme ABABCDCD, and the tercets EEFGGF. In addition, there are several run-on lines which contribute to the interplay between the complexities of the fourteen-syllable line and the variations in rhyme.

By far the most unusual use of the sonnet form, however, is to be found in "Nocturno muerto," which is a part of *Nostalgia de la muerte*:

Primero un aire tibio y lento que me ciña
como la venda al brazo enfermo de un enfermo
y que me invada luego como el silencio frío
al cuerpo desvalido y muerto de algún muerto.

Después un ruido sordo, azul y numeroso,
preso en el caracol de mi oreja dormida
y mi voz que se ahogue en ese mar de miedo
cada vez más delgada y más enardecida.

¿Quién medirá el espacio, quién me dirá el momento
en que se funda el hielo de mi cuerpo y consuma
el corazón inmóvil como la llama fría?

La tierra hecha impalpable silencioso silencio,
la soledad opaca y la sombra ceniza
caerán sobre mis ojos y afrentarán mi frente. (p. 52).

Again, the meter is Alexandrine, but one which is more subtle in its construction than "Ni la leve zozobra." The caesura which would be expected in a fourteen-syllable line is very often not marked or is nonexistent. Line 6, for example, must be read with full awareness of the *aguda* word "caracol" at the hemistich point. In addition, several run-on lines throughout the poem complicate even further the rhythmic movement of the verses. The rhyme does not fall within the classical system. It is fundamentally a system of assonance, but without strict observance of the usual rhyme sequence of the sonnet. There are two assonantal schemes, one in *i-a* and another in *é-o*, as well as four lines which are left unrhymed. The first quatrain begins all three of these interweaving patterns. It has a scheme of ABCB, line 1 establishing the *i-a* pattern, lines 2 and 4 the *é-o*, and line 3 the first of the unrhymed lines. The remainder of the rhyme pattern would then be DABABEABAF. The complexities of this sonnet lead inevitably to the conclusion already reached with other forms: Villaurrutia uses established conventions but does not follow them slavishly.

In addition to the conventional closed forms of the *décima* and the sonnet, Villaurrutia adopts in one of his poems another form which is traditional in Hispanic prosody but which is by definition an open form. The long poem "Canto a la primavera," which gives its title to the poet's last collection, is constructed in the *silva* form. There are thirteen stanzas of unequal length, ranging from combinations of thirteen lines to those of only two. The entire composition is made up of varying combinations of hendecasyllabic and heptasyllabic lines, which are the conventional meters for the *silva,* and there are only scattered assonances instead of a fixed scheme of end rhyme. The *silva* form in itself offers a great deal of liberty to the poet, and it is interesting to see that Villaurrutia uses this classical open-ended form as well as the other closed patterns which have been discussed.

Other recognizable stanza forms appear in many of Villaurrutia's poems. The couplet, for example, is used in several poems, most notably in "Deseo," from *Canto a la primavera.* Stanzas of five lines, seven lines, and eight lines also appear from time to time, though usually not as the pattern for an entire composition. None of these stanza forms approach in frequency or importance any of those already discussed.

Some mention should be made here, in addition to the brief remarks above in conjuntion with some of the stanza forms, of the most common line lengths. As might well be expected, the three most common meters are the octasyllable (the basic line in twenty-four compositions), the hendecasyllable (thirteen compositions), and the Alexandrine (thirteen compositions). There are no striking innovations in any of these meters, though at times Villaurrutia stretches conventionality by molding them to a slightly changed pattern with which he may be working. Other conventional meters, such as the heptasyllable, the eneasyllable, and the French twelve-syllable Alexandrine, appear infrequently and are confined almost entirely to *Primeros poemas.*

Non-Conventional Forms

The most convenient approach to this aspect of Villaurrutia's work is a chronological one. There are non-traditional metrics in every major collection, but there is considerable variation from one to another in frequency and type.

In *Primeros poemas* the variations from tradition take two forms. First, in what Pedro Henríquez Ureña would call "versificación irregular,"[2] there are several poems which show irregularities of stanza and line-length, but at the same time have some recognizeable form. For example, in "Le pregunté al poeta" the stanzas are of varying length, the rhyme scheme is not systematic, and the meter varies be-

---

[2] *La versificación irregular en la poesía castellana* (Madrid, RFE, 1920).

tween eleven and seven syllables. The first stanza of "Más que lento"
is another good example:

> Ya se alivia el alma mía
> trémula y amarilla;
> ya recibe la unción apasionada
> de tu mano ... Y la fría
> rigidez de mi frente,
> dulcemente entibiada,
> ya se siente ... (pp. 23-24).

The seven-line stanza form is somewhat rare in traditional Hispanic
patterns, and the wide variation of line lengths is even more uncom-
mon. Villaurrutia's combining of a four-syllable line, three seven-
syllable lines, two eight-syllable lines, and one eleven-syllable line
makes for a most unusual stanza. However, all of the line lengths
are traditional, and in that sense the stanza would be considered as
irregular versification rather than as free-verse. Finally, the rhyme
scheme in the stanza is also out of the ordinary. Lines 1 and 4 are
in consonance with each other, and line 2 is either unrhymed or in
assonance with lines 1 and 4. The remaining lines are likewise in consonance, so that the final scheme would be as follows: ab(a)Cadcd.

Some other compositions in the collection represent what can be
best described as a controlled movement toward unstopped free verse.
Recognizeable stanza forms and line lengths are used, but at the same
time there is a sense of fragmentation and flow. The composition
"Ellos y yo" is representative:

> Ellos saben vivir,
> y yo no sé,
> ya lo olvidé si lo aprendí,
> o nunca comencé ...
> Ellos saben besar,
> y yo no sé lo que es.
> Me da miedo probar
> a saber ...
> Ellos saben reír,
> Dios mío, yo no sé ...
> ¡Y tener que seguir
> así ... !
> Ellos saben hacer
> mil cosas más
> que yo no lograré

> jamás . . .
> *Ellos* saben vivir
> y reír
> y besar . . .
> *Yo*: sólo sé llorar . . . (pp. 6-7).

The poem has three stanzas of varying length and a non-systematic assonantal rhyme scheme. The most unusual aspect of the poem, however, is the unexpected sequence of lines. The base of the poem is a series of haptasyllables (a total of twelve lines are of that length) which is interrupted at one point by a nine-syllable line (line 3) and repeatedly by shorter lines. Line 2, for example, is five syllables and in the same stanza line 8 is four syllables in length. The flow of the second stanza is broken by two very short lines (12 and 16) and at the same time shows another five-syllable line (line 14). The final stanza has the opening and closing line in the basic meter, which is then in rather sharp contrast to the two interior lines which have only four syllables. The total effect of this structure is to produce the sense of sharp changes, of angular metrical units which are still under control but which contrast strikingly with conventional metrical formation.

Another example of this movement is the composition "Estío." Here the interplay of long and short lines is even more visible, and there is no discernible stanza form or rhyme scheme. The last stanza, which represents the culmination of this movement, is as follows:

> "Vámonos sin amor y sin deseo:
> sin dolor.
> Ahora que el corazón se queda
> en el frío,
> en la sombra,
> en el azul, vámonos
> va-
> mo-
> nos . . ." (p. 16).

The stanza begins with an hendecasyllabic line which is followed sharply by a four-syllable *agudo* element. The same sequence re-occurs in lines 3 and 4 of the stanza, which in turn are followed by a reverse sequence in lines 5 and 6 of a four-syllable line followed by a longer seven-syllable one. The movement of the strophe is brought sharply to a close by the division of the final three syllables of line 6 into successive two-syllable *agudo* lines, which have a spatial quality as well as a staccato auditory effect. Here again, though the line lengths are recognizeable, the movement seems to be strongly in the direction of free verse.

Reflejos shows the same variations in those poems which can be considered non-conventional. For example, "Aire" is organized in four quatrains, and, although the line length is not consistent and there is only a scattering of assonance throughout the poem, the impression is one of controlled irregularity. The lines are predominantly of eight, nine, ten, and eleven syllables, though line 4 has sixteen syllables.

By far the majority of the poems in *Reflejos* lack consistent stanza rhyme or rhythm patterns. It would be inaccurate, however, to call these poems exercises in free verse; there is still indication of control, such as punctuation, capitalization, and division into strophic units. One is tempted to see the bulk of this collection as a kind of controlled irregularity moving toward the considerably altered metrical patterns of the succeeding collections.

In "Azoteas," the house roof-tops along the street are perceived sharply against the sky as if they were sea-going vessels at a dock:

>Asoman al cielo cóncavo
>sus chimeneas
>los barcos prietos, duros,
>en este muelle
>de azoteas.
>
>Apenas si, lejos,
>un humo delgado
>mueve el horizonte . . .
>o se hinchan velas blancas
>en las cuerdas oblicuas.
>
>Sólo un reflejo quiebran
>los barcos de cartón
>en el acero
>de la ventana sumergida.
>
>Pero también el mar está en el cielo
>descorriendo largos telones
>de olas maltratadas, telones
>lentos,
>grises,
>despintados . . . (p. 40).

The poem is made up of four complete syntactical utterances, each of which begins with a capital letter, is ended by a period (in the last case there is a sense of trailing off rather than finality), and forms a complete strophe. This is an aspect of the poem which provides control, although the strophes are of varying lengths. The rhythm of the poem, however, is much more varied and unusual. There are line lengths of eleven, nine, eight, seven, six, five, four, and two syllables, and there is no visible patterning in the combination of these metrical lengths. For example, the final strophe has three longer units followed by three very short units, which underscores the thematic development of the poem at that point. Also, an insistent series of run-on lines throughout the whole poem complicates even further the widely varying combinations of the more or less conventional metrical units.

Another example is "Fonógrafos," which reads as follows:

> El silencio nos ha estrujado,
> inútiles, en los rincones.
> Y nos roe
> un retrato,
> una palabra,
> una nota.
>
> El presente y el futuro
> los inventaron
> para que no lloráramos . . .
>
> Y el corazón,
> el corazón de mica
> —sin diástole ni sístole—
> enloquece bajo la aguja
> y sangra en gritos
> su pasado. (p. 36).

Here four syntactical units are arranged in three strophes which are more or less balanced. The first and third strophes have the same number of lines, and the middle strophe is equivalent to one-half of either of the other two. There is capitalization and end punctuation, as well as the use of commas and dashes at certain important points. The line lengths vary widely, with lines of nine, eight, seven, five, and four syllables, and there is no fixed arrangement within a strophe. There is, however, an awareness of the interplay of longer and shorter lines for certain effects, as can be seen in the first stanza. Also, the

run-on lines in the various stanzas complicate the interplay between
the lines, as does also the seven-syllable line set off by dashes in the
final strophe. Again, control and experimentation are in careful balance.

A final example is the composition "Arroyo":

> ¡El sol!
> Hace trizas
> los espejos y, hechos
> azogue y vidrio,
> los empuja
> y los derrite.
>
> ¡Qué dulce el agua
> disolviendo sales!
> ¡Qué fría
> hirviendo siempre!
> ¡Cómo se astilla
> contra las piedras que esculpe!
> ¡Cómo imanta sus agujas
> rápidas!
>
> Y cómo vence luego
> el abandono
> de sus crines blancas. (p. 38).

The metrical structure of this composition is somewhat more
complex. A total of seven syntactical units are arranged in three
strophes of varying length, and both end punctuation and commas
are used throughout to provide a sense of control. The line lengths are
exceedingly varied once again, ranging from eight to two syllables,
and the complicating force of run-on lines is intensified. For example,
the first strophe has the following conformation in its six lines: 3-4-
7-5-4-5. However, if the run-on lines were to be accounted for in
the scansion, the strophe would be drastically changed.

There is an exclamatory quality to this composition which is
produced by a combination of punctuation and line arrangements,
against which certain elements of the poem serve as points of release.
The first line of the poem is set off by exclamation marks, and the
four elements of the second strophe have the same marking. This
succession of exclamatory elements builds the poem up to a point of
release in the last stanza, which though it has the same syntactical

form as the preceeding elements has no exclamation indicated in the punctuation.

In summary, then, the poems in *Reflejos* show controlled irregularity, in which usually recognizeable metrical units are combined into asystematic combinations which use conventional systems of punctuation and control.

The compositions collected under the title *Nostalgia de la muerte* represent a further step in the poet's progress toward freer metrical arrangements. There are relatively few poems that could be called regular, and there are a number without strophic patterns or punctuation which simulate a subconscious flow. There are, however, varying degrees of this sense of irregularity, and the consideration of several examples will make these differences clear.

The first composition of the collection, "Nocturno," approaches the controlled irregularity of *Reflejos*. The poem is structured in a series of six stanzas, which range in length from five to eight lines. Again there is no rhyme scheme, and the line lengths are for the most part conventional. The most frequent line length is the heptasyllable, but the poet varies this pattern considerably with lines of five, four, three, and even two syllables. Run-on lines are also very frequent in all of the strophes of the composition, with the same rhythmic complexity already discussed above. Normal punctuation is used throughout the poem; each stanza begins with a capital letter and ends with a period and there are as well other partial and complete stops indicated throughout.

There are, however, some compositions in the collection in which stanza form still exists but in which the control of punctuation has largely disappeared. "Nocturno sueño" is an example:

> Abría las salas
> profundas el sueño
> y voces delgadas
> corrientes de aire
> 5   entraban
>
> Del barco del cielo
> del papel pautado
> caía la escala
> por donde mi cuerpo
> 10   bajaba

El cielo en el suelo
como en un espejo
la calle azogada
dobló mis palabras

15 Me robó mi sombra
la sombra cerrada
Quieto de silencio
oí que mis pasos
pasaban

20 El frío de acero
a mi mano ciega
armó con su daga
Para darme muerte
la muerte esperaba

25 Y al doblar la esquina
un segundo largo
mi mano acerada
econtró mi espalda

Sin gota de sangre
30 sin ruido ni peso
a mis pies clavados
vino a dar mi cuerpo
Lo tomé en los brazos
lo llevé a mi lecho

35 Cerraba las alas
profundas el sueño (pp. 48-49).

The poem is formed in nine stanzas which range in length from two to five lines. Each stanza is opened by a capitalized word (stanzas 4 and 5 have two such capitalizations), but there is no indication throughout the poem of final stops or even partial stops indicated by commas. The poet chooses a six-syllable line as the basic metrical form of the poem, but varies it in several stanzas with a shorter three-syllable line as a closing (stanzas 1, 2, and 4). The lack of punctuation control heightens a sense of metrical flow which in turn supports the dream-like atmosphere of the poem. For example, since there is no stop indicated after "delgadas" in the first stanza, the adjective can modify in both directions, referring to "voces" and the following "corrientes." In a similar way, since there is no end stop

after the final line of stanza 1, it is possible to see a connection between the first and second stanza by reading "corrientes de aire/
entraban/Del barco del cielo/."

In a number of compositions the sense of flow is heightened even
more by a reduction or elimination of the stanza arrangement, as
well as an elimination of punctuation control. "Nocturno en que nada
se oye" is one of the best examples. There are no strophes indicated
in the poem, and the only indications of punctuation are the capital
letters at the beginning line and at about midway through the poem
(line 17), the question marks in line 12, and a single final period after
the final line. There is no scheme of rhyme, although there are some
few scattered end assonances. The sense of conventional line has vanished completely in this poem, and a free-flowing form is used instead.
Syllable lengths range from twenty (line 1) to four (line 18). The
complex rhythms of the lines ebb and flow as a part of the internal
movement which is the basic mechanism of the poem.

Canto a la primavera is much more conventional than the two
preceeding collections. There are some compositions in which more
varied forms are used, but the sense of metrical experimentation is
much reduced.

The composition which perhaps best represents this moderate
variation in form is "Estatua." [3] The poem is organized in five stanzas
which range in length from seven lines to two. There is a certain
rhythmic consistency in the poem, since the majority of the lines are
octasyllabic. There are, however, lines of four, six, and seven syllables,
which allow for a moderate sense of variation. There is no obvious
rhyme scheme, though there is scattered assonance throughout the
poem.

The conclusions that can be drawn from this discussion of conventional and non-conventional metrical forms in the poetry of
Villaurrutia are several. First, both traditional and experimental forms
exist side by side throughout the entire trajectory of the poet's works,
and at no time does one completely exclude the other. Traditional
set forms are used often, but are always adapted or changed to some
degree by the poet. At the same time, Villaurrutia's experimental and

---

[3] The poem was published in the Mexican journal *Los Sesenta* (Núm. 1,
1963). See the explanatory information there as to the dating of this composition.

non-conventional forms still show some degree of metrical control, such as stanza separation or minimal punctuation. Second, the precise proportion of conventional to non-conventional varies chronologically. The earliest and the final collections, for example, are predominantly conventional in form, while the two middle collections have a much higher proportion of metrical experimentation. Third, Villaurrutia was obviously very well-acquainted with the traditional Hispanic prosodic forms, and at the same time was very much a part of the Vanguardist movement which attempted to build a new poetic structure on the fragments of the traditional past.

Sound and Meaning

In his 1940 interview with José Luis Martínez and Alí Chumacero, Villaurrutia responded as follows to a query about his insistent use of sound patterns: "Nunca pondría en ella [la poesía] una sola palabra sin un sentido exacto o bien que fuera puramente decorativa. Si he usado de los 'juegos de palabras' es porque han sido precisos para expresar con ellos alguna idea." [4] The poet obviously did not deny the presence of these patterns in his work, but rather chose to affirm a strong relationship between sound and meaning. My examination of this aspect of Villaurrutia's verse will touch on three separate techniques: *enjambement,* alliteration, and plays on words.

The most pervasive and perhaps the most subtle technique is that of the run-on line. In almost every composition across the entire trajectory of his work, the poet makes frequent use of this device to introduce added metrical complexity and at the same time to force a relationship between metrical form and grammatical meaning. This technique has been commented on at several other points in this chapter, but other examples are in order here.

The two following stanzas are from "El viaje sin retorno" in *Primeros poemas*:

> Yo iba a ti en mi clamor, alucinante
> y alucinado, como en un irreal
> Mediterráneo, Ulises delirante.
> ¡Qué gritos en aquella soledad! ...

* * *

[4] "Con Xavier Villaurrutia," *Tierra Nueva,* I (Núm. 2, marzo-abril, 1940), 79.

> Y tú, que hoy de cordura contaminas
> la fiebre de mis sienes, y reposas
> con tu promesa mis ansias marinas
> y mi obsesión de olas ... Tú que afinas
> mis gritos y mis voces calurosas
> avivabas mi sed y ardías mi llaga. (p. 23).

By using a series of *sinalefa* linkings, it is possible to see the first stanza as an hendecasyllabic quatrain with the rhyme scheme ABAB. However, the rhythmic structure of the first three lines, which leads toward the fourth and somewhat separated hendecasyllable, is a good deal more complex. The key to that complexity is the series of run-ons which connect the first three lines and at the same time break up the conventional flow of the hendecasyllables. Looking at them from the point of view of breath groups controlled by successive *enjambement*, the three lines could be read as four elements, two of seven syllables and two of ten. The changed structure would be as follows, with the *sinalefa* and stress patterns marked:

> Yo iba a tí en mi clamór,
>
> alucinánte/y alucinádo,
>
> como en un irréal/Mediterráneo,
>
> Ulíses, delivánte.

The second stanza can be scanned as a series of five hendecasyllabic lines followed by a final dodecasyllable, with a rhyme scheme of ABAABC. Again the stanza progresses toward a final line, and is considerably complicated by a series of four successive run-on lines. Once more, as in the previous stanza, the technique of *enjambement* produces rhythmic complexities far beyond the seemingly simple succession of conventional lines.

In *Reflejos* the sense of metrical irregularity is much more pronounced, and the technique of *encabalgamiento* contributes to the development of that complexity. The last two strophes of the composition which gives title to the entire collection serve as an example:

> ¡Ay como si alguien
> golpeara en el agua,
> tu rostro se hundía
> y quebraba!

¡Ay, como si alguien
me hundiera el acero
del agua! (p. 27).

The two strophes are constructed with six-syllable lines and two
"*pie quebrado*" lines of four and three syllables. However, when the
encabalgamiento connections are made, this pattern largely disappears.
The first stanza, for example, can be seen as two groupings of eleven
and nine syllables each; the final stanza can be scanned as a single
fourteen-syllable unit.

In many of the later poems, the conventional indications of metrical control all but disappear, and it is more difficult to discuss the
connecting of one unit with another. However, even in those compositions in which there is greatest formal freedom, there is also a
sense of syntactical flow or suspension which helps to control rhythmic
movement. This segment of "Nocturno amor" is indicative:

Guardas el nombre de tu cómplice en los ojos
pero encuentro tus párpados más duros que el silencio
y antes que compartirlo matarías el goce
de entregarte en el sueño con los ojos cerrados
sufro al sentir la dicha con que tu cuerpo busca
el cuerpo que te vence más que el sueño
y comparo la fiebre de tus manos
con mis manos de hielo
y el temblor de tus sienes con mi pulso perdido (pp. 49-50).

There is a sense of movement in these lines which is not controlled
or stopped by conventional punctuation. At the same time, however,
there is still *encabalgamiento* between certain lines and a pause between others. For example, line 3 needs to be connected syntactically
with line 4, line 5 with line 6, and line 7 with line 8. Thus, even
though conventional divisions and punctuation are much reduced, the
function of run-on lines is still important.

A second technique in the relationship of sound to meaning is
that of alliteration. Though not so common as the run-on line, alliteration plays an important role in many of Villaurrutia's compositions, and reveals considerable interest on the part of the poet
in the sound of language as well as its meaning.

An early example of a poem which depends strongly on alliterative
technique is "Variaciones de colores," which comes from *Primeros*

poemas. The chromatic variation suggested in the title is supported by the varied repetitions and sonorities of the language itself. "Rojo," "gris," "amarillo" all appear more than once, and produce in their repetition a strong sense of alliteration. The final line of the first stanza in its relationship of "rojo" and "sonrojo" is both strongly alliterative and at the same time suggestive of a kind of verbal play which will be more frequent in Villaurrutia's later collections.

Villaurrutia often uses consonantal sonorities for alliterative effect in his poems. The following strophes are examples:

Sibilant:

> Todo lo que el deseo
> unta en mis labios:
> la dulzura soñada
> de un contacto,
> el sabido sabor
> de la saliva.
>
> ("Nocturno," p. 44).

Single and multiple tap:

> Nocturno mar amargo
> que circula en estrechos corredores
> de corales arterias y raíces
> y venas y medusas capilares.
>
> ("Nocturno mar," p. 60).

Nasals:

> Porque la sombra es la nieve oscura,
> la impensable callada nieve negra.
> ¡Cae la nieve sobre la noche!
>
> ("Nostalgia de la nieve," pp. 63-64).

Bilabial nasal:

> ¡Cómo pensar, un instante siquiera,
> que el hombre mortal vive!
> El hombre está muerto de miedo,
> de miedo mortal a la muerte.
>
> ("Paradoja del miedo," p. 68).

It is difficult to suggest precise thematic relationships for the alliterative patterns in Villaurrutia's poems. However, these patterns serve as a further indication of the poet's careful use of language. The musical flow of words in endless combinations is something to be admired and cultivated, and occasionally supports the conceptual development of the poem.

The third technique, and without doubt the most controversial of the three, is the repeated use of puns and word plays. Critics have defended and attacked this particular aspect of the poet's work, [5] and Villaurrutia felt the need to defend himself on several occasions. In addition to the 1940 interview, which has already been mentioned, the poet made the following interesting comments in a letter to Bernardo Ortiz de Montellano dated December 12, 1933: [6]

> ¿Se alargará excesivamente mi carta si toco el punto que me hiere más directa y personalmente? Pero, al mismo tiempo, ¡cómo rehuirlo si me está quemando los labios e impacientando entre mis dedos la pluma! Me refiero concretamente a los juegos de palabras que de un modo deliberado aparecen de vez en cuando en mis poesías como en las suyas, y cuyo uso me ha sido reprochado en silencio por más de un amigo. . . . ¿Me creerá usted si le digo que no se hallará en mis poesías un juego de palabras inmotivado o gratuito? De todos los que han acudido a una involuntaria invitación, quedan los menos, los que sirven o hago servir a mis fines. En una palabra, aquellos que mantienen, atizan o son parte del fuego de mi composición. Juego, entonces, con fuego y a riesgo de quemarme.

Villaurrutia shows himself to be sensitive to the criticisms of light-minded playfulness, and insists again in the strongest of terms that these particular patterns are deliberate and meaningful elements of his work as a whole.

The only critic to deal in any detailed way with this problem is César Rodríguez Chicharro, who in 1964 published a rather extensive article under the title "Disemia y paronomasia en la poesía de Xavier

---

[5] See among others the following: Frank Dauster, *Ensayos sobre poesía mexicana: Asedio a los Contemporáneos* (México, Andrea, 1963), pp. 19-20; Tomás Segovia, "Xavier Villaurrutia," *Revista Mexicana de Literatura* (Núm. 16-18, oct.-dic. de 1960), pp. 59-61; Arturo Torres-Rioseco, *Ensayos sobre literatura latinoamericana* (Berkeley, California Press, 1953), pp. 204-206.

[6] This letter was published along with three others as *Una botella al mar* (México, Rueca, 1946). It also appears in *Obras* under the same title, pp. 837-841. The quotation comes from the *Obras* version, pp. 840-841.

Villaurrutia." [7] Rodríguez Chicharro relates Villaurrutia to other poets and to other periods in which such rhetorical devices are used, in particular to poets of the French avant-garde and the Spanish baroque. He then develops with examples the definition of "disemia" ("doble significación") and "paronomasia" ("sonido semejante, pero significado diverso"). He has a rather careful inventory of the many occurrences of these figures in Villaurrutia's poems and concludes that the poet is as varied and as original in their use as was Góngora or any other poet with whom he might be compared. The major flaw in the study, in my opinion, is Chicharro's insistence on forcing all of the verbal plays into the two categories he proposes. I have difficulty, particularly in view of some of the examples from Villaurrutia's poems, in seeing the difference between "disemia" and "paronomasia."

My comments on these patterns take a great deal from Rodríguez Chicharro's previous work, but I approach their analysis from the point of view of technique.

Perhaps the simplest technique, and also one of the most common, is that of repetition. There are a number of verbal plays which depend on the successive reappearance of words or of phrases, sometimes in balanced patterns and other times in uneven arrangements which go against the sense of pattern. For example, the following lines have a visible sense of balance and arrangement:

> dónde empieza o acaba, ni si empieza o acaba.
> ("Nocturno," p. 53)

> No, no es la rosa rosa
> ("Nocturno rosa," p. 58)

> El mar que hace un trabajo lento y lento
> ("Nocturno mar," p. 59)

On the other hand, some repetitive patterns are decidedly uneven, and approximate in their movement a sense of subconscious flow. The following two lines are indicative:

> y contar a su oreja cien veces cien cien veces
> ("Nocturno de la estatua, p. 47)

---

[7] *La Palabra y el Hombre,* (abril-junio de 1964), 249-260.

cuando la vi cuando la vid cuando la vida
("Nocturno eterno," p. 51)

A times the repetitions depend on the use of the same words in two different grammatical constructions, as the following examples show:

como la venda al brazo enfermo de un enfermo

* * *

al cuerpo desvalido y muerto de algún muerto.
("Nocturno muerto," p. 52).

A second technique, and the one perhaps most affected by what Villaurrutia has called the "demonio de las analogías," [8] is the relating of similar elements through the use of closely related words. At times these patterns are of relatively small thematic or aesthetic effect, as the following examples indicate:

y rojo tu sonrojo.
("Variaciones de colores," p. 12)

La tierra hecha impalpable silencioso silencio,
("Nocturno muerto," p. 52)

olvidos olvidados y deseos,
("Nocturno mar," p. 59)

At times, however, the relationships formed with this technique are more striking and at the same time important for the development of the poem. For example, the line "la rosa de rosadas uñas" ("Nocturno rosa," p. 58) is an integral and important part of the long succession of strange but substantial images built up on the stereotyped rose. Also, the pattern seen in the line "me estoy mirando mirarme por mil Argos," ("Poesía," p. 26) heightens notably the sense of multiple and penetrating scrutiny which is a fundamental part of the poem.

---

[8] *Obras,* p. 841.

A similar technique is that of relating elements through the use of words or signs which are similar in appearance or sound but which are not necessarily closely related. The following lines are examples:

> Tu voz, hoz de eco,
>> ("Poesía," p. 26)

> la rosa entraña
> que se pliega y expande
> evocada, invocada, abocada,
>> ("Nocturno rosa," p. 58)

> Nocturno mar amargo
>> ("Nocturno mar," p. 60)

> entre las incansables
> eternas olas altas.
>> ("Canto a la primavera," p. 74).

There is a unique example of this technique which needs further comment. The first strophe of the composition "Pueblo," from *Reflejos,* uses at one point signs instead of words:

> Aquel pueblo se quedó soltero,
> conforme con su iglesia,
> embozado en su silencio,
> bajo la paja —oro, mediodía—
> de su sombrero ancho,
> sin nada más:
> en las fichas del comentario
> los + son—. (p. 34).

The plus and minus signs of the final line can be seen as a part of the visual depiction of a small village with its church and cemetery. The plus sign can represent the crosses marking each grave or niche, and the minus sign the grouping of those burial places into neat rows. If the signs are read as mathematical indications, "más" and "menos," they can just as well express an ironic view of life and death: in the sleepy silence of a small-town cemetery all positive qualities are made negative and all men are the same.

Another technique which is very productive of word plays is the shifting of stress patterns or word boundaries so as to create two elements which are related and at the same time separate. Nearly all of the examples which critics point out as characteristic of Villaurrutia's work are of this type. Within this general classification, however, there are several distinct sub-classes.

Some of the verbal plays are produced by the orthographic marking of a verbal or adverbial form:

> el latido de un mar en el que no sé nada
> en el que no se nada
> > ("Nocturno en que nada se oye," p. 47)

> Y solo, sólo yo sé que la muerte
> > ("Nocturno de la alcoba," p. 61)

Some other patterns depend on the shifting of word boundaries, occasionally coupled with slight changes in phonemes or orthography:

> sin más pulso ni voz y sin más cara,
> sin máscara como un hombre desnudo
> > ("Poesía," p. 26)

> Abría las salas
> profundas el sueño
>
> > * * *
>
> Cerraba las alas
> profundas el sueño
> > ("Nocturno sueño," pp. 48-49)

> ¿Quién medirá el espacio, quién me dirá el momento
> > ("Nocturno muerto," p. 52).

Some other patterns combine shifting of boundaries with spelling changes and changes in capitalization, and produce the impression of heightened complexity:

> me estoy mirando mirarme por mil Argos,
> por mí largos segundos.
> > ("Poesía," p. 26)

> En Boston es grave falta
> hablar de ciertas mujeres,
> por eso aunque nieva nieve
> mi boca no se atreve

a decir en voz alta:
ni Eva ni Hebe.

("Epigramas de Boston," p. 89).

Villaurrutia's best known play on words is one which uses the technique being discussed here. The passage is a part of "Nocturno en que nada se oye":

> Y en el juego angustioso de un espejo frente a otro
> cae mi voz
> y mi voz que madura
> y mi voz quemadura
> y mi bosque madura
> y mi voz quema dura
> como el hielo de vidrio (p. 47).

The basic mechanism is that of shifting of boundaries to produce a series of different grammatical combinations. With several shifts of limits and a change of one consonant the poet uses the same elements to produce the following grammatical scheme: noun + conjunction + verb/noun + adjective/noun + verb/noun + verb + adverb.

The arrangement is ingenious, and its obvious manipulation of elements has been much debated. The poet does use the term "juego" in the first line of the passage, but it is an anguished game and he is completely serious. In my opinion the word play is successful in producing the sense of endless echoing of mirror images which the poem demands at that point.

In addition to the techniques discussed up to this point, there are two others which are less frequent but nonetheless need to be mentioned here. The first of these, a favorite technique with other vanguardist poets, [9] is the coining of a word which by false analogy seems to have a relationship with some other element in the poem, or the forcing of a further dimension in a word in current usage. The line "la rosa del insomnio desojada." ("Nocturno rosa," p. 58) is an example. The word "desojada" does not exist, and its invention here

---

[9] The following lines from Vicente Huidobro's *Altazor* (*Obras completas,* Vol. 1, Santiago de Chile, Zig-Zag, 1964) serve as a more extreme example:

> El meteoro insolente cruza por el cielo
> El meteplata el metecobre
> El metepiedras en el infinito
> Meteópalos en la mirada (p. 401).

makes possible the play between "rosa deshojada" and the relationship of "ojo" to sleep and the insomniac who stares fixedly at the shapes of the night. Another example is the sequence "Mar sin viento ni cielo,/sin olas, desolado," ("Nocturno mar," p. 59). Here the term "desolado" does exist in the language, but not with one of the meanings which the poet gives it, that of being without waves, or "dewaved." The resulting pun is one in which the poet forces a new meaning to indicate a sense of anguished desolation. One final example is a curious play which depends on the "seseo" in Mexican Spanish: "mas huye todo como el pez que se da cuenta/hasta ciento en el pulso de mis sienes/muda telegrafía a la que nadie responde ("Nocturno en que nada se oye," p. 48). Here the sense of double direction from the same base is produced by a counting toward one hundred ("ciento") and at the same time by the pronunciation of the word ("siento") which moves the image toward a telegraphic system which no one answers.

The second minor technique is that of a reversal of set patterns. The poet creates a sense of verbal play at times by reversing or intertwining phrases which have become clichés in the language. Some examples are as follows:

y contar a su oreja cien veces cien cien veces
hasta oírla decir: "estoy muerta de sueño."

("Nocturno de la estatua," p. 47)

y a unirnos y a estrecharnos, más que solos y náufragos,
todavía más, y cada vez más, todavía.

("Nocturno de la alcoba," p. 61)

Y comprendo de una vez para nunca
el clima del silencio

("Muerte en el frío," p. 67).

These reversal patterns are in general less important than the double-meaning passages already discussed, but at the same time are a further indication of the poet's awareness of the unexpected and hidden complexities of poetic language.

Summary

Certain important conclusions are clear in regard to this aspect of Villaurrutia's poetry. First, it is apparent that the poet was familiar with traditional Spanish versification as well as with the experimental currents of his time. Patterned forms are used often, but never with absolute conventionality. Experimentation is also frequent, but again seldom with the sense of complete freedom which characterizes other poets of the same period. Second, Villaurrutia was very much aware of the acoustical and musical dimensions of poetic language, and took full advantage of these qualities in the construction of his poems. The techniques of *enjambement,* alliteration, and word plays are important focal points of this preoccupation. Third, there is no basis for seeing Villaurrutia's work as primarily decorative or playful. With one or two possible exceptions the poet's use of metrics, sound, and puns is serious, and, as the poet himself has indicated, is a functional part of the presentation of a complex poetic structure.

CHAPTER IV

IMAGERY AND SYMBOL

The Collections

The imagery of *Primeros poemas,* Villaurrutia's adolescent verses (all written and published before the poet was twenty), is strongly external. In most of the compositions the elements of a recognizable natural world are clearly visible, and a very Modernistic infatuation with objects and colors can be seen as well:

> Y el crepúsculo rojo que a lo lejos moría
> en su último rútilo al hundirse en lo arcano
> iluminó mi rostro. Yo sentí que vivía
> y la besé en la frente, y la besé en la mano.
>
> ("En la tarde que muere ...," p. 3)

> Visión de la lluvia, la de manos yertas
> que parecen lilas marchitas o muertas!
>
> ("La visión de la lluvia," p. 11)

> Yo persigo, sentado al borde de la fuente,
> la calma que mitique mi avidez de recuerdo
> y brilla entre mis labios el rojo que no siente
> el sangrar de una rosa que distraído muerdo.
>
> ("Remanso," p. 13).

This is not to suggest that all of these poems are a stilted imitation of Modernism. At times the young poet is able to break away from clichéd images and achieve descriptive poetry of unexpected brilliance. An example is the composition "Tarde":

Un maduro perfume de membrillo en las ropas
blancas y almidonadas ... ¡Oh campestre saludo
del ropero asombrado, que nos abre sus puertas
sin espejos, enormes y de un tallado rudo! ...

Llena el olor la alcoba, mientras el sol afuera
camina poco a poco, se duplica en la noria,
bruñe cada racimo, cada pecosa pera,
y le graznan los patos su rima obligatoria.

En todo se deslíe el perfume a membrillo
que salió de la alcoba ... Es como una oración
que supimos de niños ... Si —como el corderillo
prófugo del redil— huyó de la memoria,
hoy, que a nosotros vuelve, se ensancha el corazón.

Dulzura hay en el alma, y juventud, y vida,
y perfume en la tarde que, ya desvanecida,
se va tornando rosa, dejando la fragancia
de la ropa que vela, mientras muere la estancia ... (p. 16).

The imagery in this poem is highly sensorial, and is the principal
vehicle in the description of a sunny afternoon in the country. The
first strophe, for example, represents the quince-like smell of freshly
starched and pressed clothing (with perhaps tactile and auditory suggestions), and the strong visual contrast represented by the whiteness
of the clothes and the "ropero" in which they are kept. The second
stanza continues the olfactory imagery, and at the same time presents
a series of things which are happening outside the house. The sun
moves slowly in its path until it is reflected in the waters of the
well, and at the same time leaves its imprint on everything it touches.
The line "bruñe cada racimo, cada pecosa pera,", in addition to its
alliterative quality, represents a very effective visual image. [1] The
third stanza again uses the odor of quince, but here to compare it to

---

[1] Villaurrutia records a conversation with Ramón López Velarde in which
the older poet singles out this line for comment: "El sol en su trayectoria,
visto fuera y dentro de la casa, era el personaje del poema y el sujeto del
verso debajo del que amplificado, enorme, vi resbalar lenta y pendularmente
el índice de la mano derecha de Ramón López Velarde, al tiempo que decía:
'Es extraordinario cómo ha captado usted estas dos cosas. En efecto, el sol
bruñe, ésa es la palabra, los racimos. ¡Y qué definitivamente retratadas por
usted quedan las peras, no sólo por el lustre, sino también y precisamente,
por las pecas! Eso es: las peras son pecosas.' " (*Obras*, p. 643).

a child's prayer, which like a wandering lamb returns and brings
about a feeling of joy. The last stanza combines the declarative first
line with the smells of the afternoon and of the starched clothing
within the room as the light of the afternoon changes and dies. The
imagery in the poem is multifaceted and leads backward toward
the memory of youth, but it is also a rather objective representation
of the internal and external elements of the scene being portrayed.

Another interesting example of a poem in which the imagery is
no longer imitative is "Variaciones de colores":

> Rojo y gris,
> verde y rojo,
> y amarillo el tapiz
> y rojo tu sonrojo.
>
> Es este cielo gris,
> la calzada de un rojo
> húmedo, hojas muertas,
> amarillo el tapiz
> y verdes las ramas alertas ...
>
> Tu corazón es rojo,
> mi pensamiento gris,
> amarillo el crepúsculo,
> amarillo el tapiz. (p. 12).

This poem has already been commented on as alliterative repetition, but it also makes notable use of chromatic imagery. The first
stanza presents several contrasting colors and relates one of them,
"rojo," to a familiar "tú". In the second stanza the same colors are
applied to different things ("cielo gris", "calzada roja", "ramas
verdes"), and only the line "amarillo el tapiz" remains the same. The
stanza becomes a kind of scenic representation in which the gray sky
extends over an autumnal scene of dead leaves, stark branches, and
the red color of a path or street.

The third stanza connects the "rojo" with the "tú", the gray of
the sky with the "yo" of the poem, and the repeated "amarillo" in the
final line becomes the closing sense impression of the entire composition.

The starkness of the chromatic representation is not like the
delicate shadings of the Modernist style, and the seemingly deliberate

vagueness in the significance of some of the images (the yellow carpet, for example, or the red dampness of the road) anticipates many of the characteristics of Villaurrutia's later poems.

"Esta música" is another composition in which the placid surface of a benign natural world is ruffled:

> Esta música tan sencilla
> ya no sé por qué me conmueve.
> Hasta los árboles se inclinan
> como se inclinan cuando llueve.
>
> Yo no quiero mirar al ciego . . .
> Su violín es rudimentario,
> pero las notas, aunque agudas,
> no se han nunca desafinado.
>
> Yo comprendo que el viejo llora,
> su música lo hace sentir . . .
> Serán sus ojos todo blanco,
> no lo veo, no lo quiero oír . . .
>
> Interminable la balada
> que arranca del pobre violín,
> interminable mi congoja.
> ¡Oh!, puede que no tenga fin . . . (pp. 12-13).

Here the imagery captures perfectly, in visual and auditory terms, the scene of a blind beggar playing a primitive violin on the street. The imagery of the successive stanzas leads inevitably to the statements of the final stanza, which represent first the endlessness of the musical sound and then the endlessness of the anguish which the whole experience produces in the auditor. Thus, the movement of the imagery is from external simplicity to internal emotional turbulence, a direction which will be apparent often in Villaurrutia's later compositions.

In summary, then, *Primeros poemas* must be seen as the poet's exercises of adolescence; in general these reflect the lessons learned from Modernism and some of its major figures. At the same time, however, there are poems which represent considerable originality on the part of the poet, and which mark major directions which will be taken in later collections.

The imagery of *Reflejos*, the first collection of poems organized and published by the poet himself, is significantly different. There

is still an evident desire to communicate an external reality related
to an internal emotional state, and widely varied chromatic and
sensorial images are used in this presentation. However, whereas in
Primeros poemas external reality was essentially simple and stable,
in *Reflejos* that reality is fragmented and ever-changing. A particular
moment or scene can be contemplated from a number of points of
view:

> Vámonos inmóviles de viaje
> para ver la tarde de siempre
> con otra mirada,
> para ver la mirada de siempre
> con distinta tarde.
>
> Vámonos, inmóviles.
>
> > ("Lugares [I]," p. 33).

The longer composition "Reflejos," which gives title to the entire
collection, is also an example of this view of reality and poetic description:

> Eras como el agua
> un rostro movido, ¡ay!,
> cortado
> por el metal de los reflejos.
>
> Yo te quería sola,
> asomada a la fuente de los días,
> y tan muda y tan quieta
> en medio del paisaje móvil:
> húmedas ramas y nubes delgadas.
>
> Y sólo en un momento
> te me dabas, mujer.
> Eso era cuando el agua
> como que ensamblaba
> sus planos azules,
> un instante inmóvil,
> para luego hundirlos
> entre rayas blancas
> de sol, y moradas.
>
> ¡Ay como si alguien
> golpeara en el agua,
> tu rostro se hundía
> y quebraba!

> ¡Ay, como si alguien
> me hundiera el acero
> del agua! (p. 27).

As is suggested by the title, the basic image sequence in the poem is that of a remembered, reflected, view of a beloved person. The simile of the first stanza, in past tense and with the sharp metallic separations of various reflections, communicates the impossibility of exact remembrance. The following two stanzas continue this general representation, seen first as quiet and mobile in its reflection and then something captured only momentarily in a flash of brilliant reflected rays. The fourth stanza takes again the moving reflection of the beloved's face on the well of memory, only to see it shatter and sink as if a stone had been dropped into the limpid pool. The final stanza returns to the metallic imagery which was begun in the first, and combines it with the reflective imagery of the succeeding stanzas. The effect of the final stanza is that of making the entire image sequence of the poem a dagger which pierces the sensibility of the onlooker.

There are a number of compositions which use the device of a picture, a mirror, or a frame in order to capture momentarily the passing scene:

> El aire que vuelve de un viaje,
> lleno de dorado calor,
> se hiela en un marco para ser espejo
> y cuadro de comedor.
>> ("Interior," p. 30)

> La moldura de la ventana
> rebana un trozo de jardín.

> Hasta el aire con marco de los cristales
> mueve el mismo temblor que mueve el velo
> de la danza primaveral.
>> ("Jardín," p. 32).

Even in the poems which most obviously depict "still life" and the stylized representation of an Impressionist painting, there is still a marked sense of suspended movement and energy. The poem "Cézanne" is perhaps the best example:

> Deshace julio en vapor los cristales
> de las ventanas del agua y del aire.

En el blanco azul tornasol del mantel
los frutos toman posturas eternas
para el ojo y para el pincel.

Junto a las naranjas de abiertos poros
las manzanas se pintan demasiado,
y a los duraznos, por su piel de quince años,
dan deseos de acariciarlos.
Los perones rodaron su mármol transparente
lejos de las peras pecosas
y de las nueces arrugadas.

¡Calor! Sin embargo, da pena
beberse la "naturaleza muerta"
que han dejado dentro del vaso. (p. 31).

The basic sequence of imagery sets up a frame in the first stanza and then depicts a stylized still life "para el ojo y para el pincel." However, it is notable that the representation of the still life is suggested as being something which was brought to completion at that moment and once the "posturas" are finished, will dissolve. The verbs "deshace" in line 1, "toman" in line 3, "rodaron" in line 10, and "han dejado" in the final line all have a suggestion of movement which is contrary to the frozen figures of the moment.

Another interesting representation of the depiction and destruction of a changing reality is "Puzzle":

Cuando subimos por sus rodillas
gruñó un poco:
su aliento silvó en su cabellera verde,
y tuvimos miedo . . .
Pero no cambió de postura.

Cuando pisábamos su espalda
miramos hacia abajo:
Navidad en abril.
Absurdo: esa cabra, ese buey,
los hombres hongos
y el espejito roto entre la lama.

Arriba comprendimos
que sin esfuerzo, con una mano,
podríamos derribarlo todo:
casas, árboles,

> hasta la vaca pinta
> segura de su *camouflage*.
> ¡Todo! Con ademán de niño
> aburrido y enfermo:
> ya lo ordenaríamos después,
> o ya nunca lo ordenaríamos. (pp. 35-36).

The title suggests the basic image pattern of the poem. This is a landscape, seen not horizontally but from above, which in turn permits a view much like a jig-saw puzzle. The first stanza represents, in highly personified terms, the climbing of a hill or mountain from which the countryside can subsequently be seen. In the second stanza the top is reached and the landscape is spread out below, as if it were a set of toys or dolls at Christmas time. Cattle, streams, fields, and even men (who with their tall hats appear to be in the shape of mushrooms when seen from above), are all absurdly small. The third stanza represents the opposite facet of the imagery in the poem. Here the poet realizes that with one gesture, he can, as would a child bored with his new toys, scatter the elements of the scene to gather them up or not as he pleases. Here again, reality being viewed is not something stable but something transitory which can be destroyed and reconstituted at the pleasure of the poet.

At times carefully constructed imagery will move a poem from an initial external reality to a figurative one, a process which again suggests the progressive instability of the external world. In "Azoteas," for example, the chimneys and roof-tops of the city become, through the use of an extended metaphor, black ships tied to a dock:

> Asoman al cielo cóncavo
> sus chimeneas
> los barcos prietos, duros,
> en este muelle
> de azoteas.
>
> Apenas si, lejos,
> un humo delgado
> mueve el horizonte...
> o se hinchan velas blancas
> en las cuerdas oblicuas. (p. 40).

In summary, then, the imagery of *Reflejos* is one in which external reality is seen as something fragile and momentary which can be recaptured only fleetingly through the careful use of figurative language.

Villaurrutia has given the title of "Nocturnos" to most of the compositions collected in *Nostalgia de la muerte,* and this term describes the essence of the collection. Here the break with external reality is almost complete, and in contrast to the fragmented and sensorial brilliance of preceeding poems, the imagery of the *nocturnos* leads downward into a shadowy and subterranean world:

> En la noche resuena, como en un mundo hueco,
> el ruido de mis pasos prolongados, distantes.
> Siento miedo de que no sea sino el eco
> de otros pasos ajenos, que pasaron mucho antes.
>
> ("Estancias nocturnas," p. 62)

> Soledad, aburrimiento,
> vano silencio profundo,
> líquida sombra en que me hundo,
> vacío del pensamiento.
> Y ni siquiera el acento
> de una voz indefinible
> que llegue hasta el imposible
> rincón de un mar infinito
> a iluminar con su grito
> este naufragio invisible.
>
> ("Nocturno solo," pp. 50-51)

The momentary recapturing of a face or a landscape is gone, and in its place are insistent images which turn in on themselves to represent not substantial form but only shapes and shadows. Where there was once day there is now night, where there was once life there is now only death, and where there was once physical presence there is now only an empty place. The cold and the shadows are so intense that they become stronger and more painful than the realities which they represent:

> De qué noche despierto a esta desnuda
> noche larga y cruel noche que ya no es noche
> junto a tu cuerpo más muerto que muerto
> que no es tu cuerpo ya sino su hueco
> porque la ausencia de tu sueño ha matado a la muerte
> y es tan grande mi frío que con un calor nuevo
> abre mis ojos donde la sombra es más dura

y más clara y más luz que la luz misma
y resucita en mí lo que no ha sido
y es un dolor inesperado y aún más frío y más fuego
no ser sino la estatua que despierta
en la alcoba de un mundo en el que todo ha muerto.

("Nocturno amor," p. 50).

The representation of this intensified and anguished world brings with it some changes and reductions in imagery. For example, chromatic imagery appears much less frequently in *Nostalgia de la muerte* than in the preceeding collections, and when it is used it is generally as a reduced contrastive system (darkness against light, black against white, etc.). This stanza from "Nostalgia de la nieve" is a good example:

Y algo de dulce sueño,
de sueño sin angustia,
infantil, tierno, leve
goce no recordado
tiene la milagrosa
forma en que por la noche
caen las silenciosas
sombras blancas de nieve. (p. 64).

There is reduction and sharpening in other kinds of imagery as well. The representation of heat and cold, for example, tends to lose any kind of shading and takes strongly the quality of destruction and consummation by fire or the paralysis and congealing effects of cold. The three following stanzas from "Muerte en el frío" serve as examples:

siento que estoy en el infierno frío,
en el invierno eterno
que congela la sangre en las arterias,
que seca las palabras amarillas,
que paraliza el sueño,
que pone una mordaza de hielo a nuestra boca
y dibuja las cosas con una línea dura.

Siento que estoy viviendo aquí mi muerte,
mi sola muerte presente,
mi muerte que no puedo compartir ni llorar,
mi muerte de que no me consolaré jamás.

Y comprendo de una vez para nunca
el clima del silencio
donde se nutre y perfecciona la muerte.
Y también la eficacia del frío
que preserva y purifica sin consumir como el fuego. (p. 67).

One of the most interesting poems in the collection from the point of view of imagery is "Nocturno rosa," [2] which makes use of a stereotyped poetic object in the imagery of incompleteness and emptiness which is a part of this collection:

Yo también hablo de la rosa.
Pero mi rosa no es la rosa fría
ni la de piel de niño,
ni la rosa que gira
5   tan lentamente que su movimiento
es una misteriosa forma de la quietud.

No es la rosa sedienta,
ni la sangrante llaga,
ni la rosa coronada de espinas,
10   ni la rosa de la resurrección.

No es la rosa de pétalos desnudos,
ni la rosa encerada,
ni la llama de seda,
ni tampoco la rosa llamarada.

15   No es la rosa veleta,
ni la úlcera secreta,
ni la rosa puntual que da la hora,
ni la brújula rosa marinera.

No, no es la rosa rosa
20   sino la rosa increada,
la sumergida rosa,
la nocturna,
la rosa inmaterial,
la rosa hueca.

---

* In many places this title is indicated "Nocturna rosa," which in many ways is just as much in keeping with the central imagery of the poem. However, I am unable to determine whether this variant title can be attributed to a mistake of an editor, or whether it is another of the poet's puns.

25 Es la rosa del tacto en las tinieblas,
    es la rosa que avanza enardecida,
    la rosa de rosadas uñas,
    la rosa yema de los dedos ávidos,
    la rosa digital,
30 la rosa ciega.

    Es la rosa moldura del oído,
    la rosa oreja,
    la espiral del ruido,
    la rosa concha siempre abandonada
35 en la más alta espuma de la almohada.

    Es la rosa encarnada de la boca,
    la rosa que habla despierta
    como si estuviera dormida.
    Es la rosa entreabierta
40 de la que mana sombra,
    la rosa entraña
    que se pliega y expande
    evocada, invocada, abocada,
    es la rosa labial,
45 la rosa herida.

    Es la rosa que abre los párpados,
    la rosa vigilante, desvelada,
    la rosa del insomnio desojada.

    Es la rosa del humo,
50 la rosa de ceniza,
    la negra rosa de carbón diamante
    que silenciosa horada las tinieblas
    y no ocupa lugar en el espacio. (pp. 57-58).

The imagery of the poem depicts the rose in two opposing aspects: denial and affirmation or perhaps simply negative and positive. The first four stanzas represent the negative, in which successive images having to do with the shape or color of the rose are linked together by a series of negative words. The view of the rose in its superficial colors, shapes, and textures is denied as far as the poet is concerned, even in those images which suggest warmth (line 14), religious hope (line 10), or a sense of direction (line 18).

Stanza 5 is the pivotal point of the imagery in the poem. Line 19 sums up the preceeding stanzas, and the remaining lines which follow present the basic image for the stanzas which are to come. The rose which is important for the poet is one which is outside natural creation, one which is nocturnal, submerged, and empty of conventional form and shape. The remaining five stanzas of the poem develop the affirmative, and are interconnected by a series of present indicative verbs. The rose is represented first as a series of tactile images, blind in the visual sense but very much alive to the sense of touch. Auditory perception is also sharpened, and even during sleep the sounds of the surrounding world enter the subconscious. The mouth speaks, not from the organized substance of conscious reality but rather as if it were asleep, speaking from a deep dream state. The rose is a vigilant insomniac that above all maintains the sharpened sensorial perception and the heightened feeling of anguish which is often associated with a dream. The final stanza summarizes, again in insubstantial chromatic and tactile terms, the rose of which the poet speaks. It is the color and consistency of smoke, it is ashen, it has the hardness and capacity for penetration of the star bit of a diamond drill. And finally, it is so insubstantial that it occupies space only within the consciousness of the poet.

The imagery of the poem is carefully conceived and executed, and in its complex interlayering of reality and irreality, it is typical of the imagery of *Nostalgia de la muerte*. In a studied fashion, the negative segment of the poem denies positive reality, and the positive segment affirms a negative and unmaterial irreality.

The imagery of *Canto a la primavera y otros poemas,* the last collection of Villaurrutia's verses, evidences still another direction. The lonely nocturnal galleries of *Nostalgia de la muerte* have faded, and the images here suggest, to turn Darío's famous title completely around, a fleeting reminiscence of spring amidst an onrushing autumn:

> Porque la primavera
> es ante todo la verdad primera,
> la verdad que se asoma
> sin ruido, en un momento,
> la que al fin nos parece
> que va a durar, eterna,
> la que desaparece
> sin dejar otra huella
> que la que deja el ala
> de un pájaro en el viento.

("Canto a la primavera," p. 76).

The imagery of the collection, however, does not return to the Impressionistic shadings of *Reflejos,* but rather retains much of the obsessive concentration already discussed in connection with *Nostalgia de la muerte.* The driving force behind these verses is the expression of a hidden and impossible love, and the same reductions and concentrations of sensorial language already commented on in the preceeding collection often operate here to express this impossible emotion. The final *décima* from "Décimas de nuestro amor" is an example of such a use of thermic and visual imagery:

> Mi amor por ti ¡no murió!
> Sigue viviendo en la fría,
> ignorada galería
> que en mi corazón cavó.
> Por ella desciendo y no
> encontraré la salida,
> pues será toda mi vida
> esta angustia de buscarte
> a ciegas, con la escondida
> certidumbre de no hallarte. (p. 82).

The image of a secret space in which love is imprisoned and is formed little by little is often repeated in the collection. The process of this love can be compared, for example, to increasing sweetness within the shadowy and florescent cavern of a ripening fig: "Amor secreto que convierte en miel la sombra,/como la florescencia en la cárcel del higo." (p. 84). A more extensive use of the same imagery is "Soneto de la granada":

> Es mi amor como el oscuro
> panal de sombra encarnada,
> que la hermética granada
> labra en su cóncavo muro.
>
> Silenciosamente apuro
> mi sed, mi sed no saciada,
> y la guardo congelada
> para un alivio futuro.
>
> Acaso una boca ajena
> a mi secreto dolor
> encuentre mi sangre, plena,

y mi carne, dura y fría,
y en mi acre y dulce sabor
sacie su sed con la mía. (p. 78).

The principal system of imagery here is provided by the peculiar form of the pomegranate, which is single and multiple, external and internal at the same time. The poet's love is internalized and is stored experience by experience inside the concavity of his consciousness as are individual garnet kernels within the pomegranate. His thirst for love, never fully satisfied, is frozen and kept in the hope that his suffering may solace some future reader. The poet's essence is expressed by the potential liquidity of the fruit, which in turn may assuage the passion of unrequited love as physical thirst is slaked by the pomegranate.

The imagery of many of the poems suggests the silences, the doubts, the strong emotions, and the impossibilities of this secret and barely expressed love. These stanzas from "Amor condusse noi ad una morte" are typical:

Amar es una angustia, una pregunta,
una suspensa y luminosa duda;
es un querer saber todo lo tuyo
y a la vez un temor de al fin saberlo.

Amar es reconstruir, cuando te alejas,
tus pasos, tus silencios, tus palabras,
y pretender seguir tu pensamiento
cuando a mi lado, al fin inmóvil, callas.

Amar es una cólera secreta,
una helada y diabólica soberbia. (p. 76).

The imagery of *Canto a la primavera*, then, is impassioned but turned in upon itself, depicting an internal structure which is intricate and sensorial, but which cannot be brought out onto the surface. The images of unrequited love are desperate and hidden, and express the impossibility of emotion which is realized and complete.

Image Patterns, Motifs, and Symbols

Four groupings of images, together with some related motifs and symbols, are of particular importance: 1) images of sleeping and dreaming; 2) images which reflect an internal-external contrast; 3) images making use of the human body; 4) images of liquidity. All of these groupings extend beyond the limits of a single collection, and therefore need to be examined outside the chronological framework established in the first part of the chapter.

Sleeping and Dreaming

A state of sleeping or dreaming, in which the poet is liberated from the forms of the external world, is frequently found in Villaurrutia's poems. This process is represented at times in accoustical and aquatic terms:

> Te forman las palabras
> que salen del silencio
> y del tanque de sueño en que me ahogo
> libre hasta despertar.
>
> (*Reflejos,* "Poesía," p. 26).

In sleep the limits of the conscious world are destroyed:

> en esta soledad sin paredes
> al tiempo que huyeron los ángulos
> en la tumba del lecho dejo mi estatua sin sangre
> para salir en un momento tan lento
> en un interminable descenso
>
> ("Nocturno en que nada se oye," p. 47).

The heightened subconscious then, with the uncertain gait of a sleepwalker, moves without limitation and without fixed purpose:

> Entonces, con el paso de un dormido despierto,
> sin rumbo y sin objeto nos echamos a andar.
> La noche vierte sobre nosotros su misterio,
> y algo nos dice que morir es despertar.
>
> ("Nocturno miedo," p. 45).

There are two important motifs in the representation of this dream state, the personified night and the nocturnal street. The night, for example, is often represented as a shadowy human figure who blots out with her shadows the conscious realities of the world and makes apparent those desires which lie beneath the surface:

Todo lo que la noche
dibuja con su mano
de sombra:
el placer que revela,
el vicio que desnuda.

("Nocturno," p. 44).

cuando la tarde, al fin, ha recogido
el último destello de luz, la última nube,
el reflejo olvidado y el ruido interrumpido,
la noche surge silenciosamente
de ranuras secretas,
de rincones ocultos,
de bocas entreabiertas,
de ojos insomnes.

La noche surge con el humo denso
del cigarrillo y de la chimenea.
La noche surge envuelta en su manto de polvo.

("Cuando la tarde . . . ," p. 62).

Perhaps the best example of the use of this motif is the composition "Nocturno":

Al fin llegó la noche con sus largos silencios,
con las húmedas sombras que todo lo amortiguan.
El más ligero ruido crece de pronto y, luego,
muere sin agonía.

5　El oído se aguza para ensartar un eco
lejano, o el rumor de unas voces que dejan,
al pasar, una huella de vocales perdidas.

¡Al fin llegó la noche tendiendo cenicientas
alfombras, apagando luces, ventanas últimas!

10　Porque el silencio alarga lentas manos de sombra.
La sombra es silenciosa, tanto que no sabemos
dónde empieza o acaba, ni si empieza o acaba.

Y es inútil que encienda a mi lado una lámpara:
la luz hace más honda la mina del silencio
15　y por ella desciendo, inmóvil, de mí mismo.

Al fin llegó la noche a despertar palabras
ajenas, desusadas, propias, desvanecidas:
tinieblas, corazón, misterio, plenilunio . . .

¡Al fin llegó la noche, la soledad, la espera!
20   Porque la noche es siempre el mar de un sueño antiguo,
de un sueño hueco y frío en el que ya no queda
del mar sino los restos de un naufragio de olvidos.

Porque la noche arrastra en su baja marea
memorias angustiosas, temores congelados,
25   la sed de algo que, trémulos, apuramos un día,
y la amargura de lo que ya no recordamos.

¡Al fin llegó la noche a inundar mis oídos
con una silenciosa marea inesperada,
a poner en mis ojos unos párpados muertos,
a dejar en mis manos un mensaje vacío! (pp. 53-54).

The poem revolves around an extended metaphor of night which
is introduced consistently by the anaphoric phrase "Al fin llegó" (lines
1, 8, 16, 19, and 27). Night is a shadowy figure who with damp
shrouds and ashen carpets puts out the light of the world and intro-
duces a state of silence or darkness. The night, continuing as a personified entity, whispers forgotten words which awaken emotions long
since left behind. Night then becomes a sea, which in its ebbing and
flowing reveals those anguishes and fears which are normally covered
by the waters of the day. In the final stanza night is both a flood
which overwhelms and drowns and also the same imprecise presence which leaves an empty message in the hands of the poet. The
careful creation of a personified and changing night, which with its
onrushing and revealing presence produces intensified awareness, is an
important part of the representation of the dream state in Villaurrutia's
poems, and here, at least, symbolizes the destructive force of death
against life and experience.

The second motif related to this image system is that of the nocturnal street. At times the street is deserted, and is representative of
the moment in which each man comes face to face with himself:

¿Y quién entre las sombras de una calle desierta,
en el muro, lívido espejo de soledad,
no se ha visto pasar o venir a su encuentro
y no ha sentido miedo, angustia, duda mortal?
("Nocturno miedo," p. 45).

The street may take the form of a river:

De pronto el río de la calle se puebla de sedientos seres,
caminan, se detienen, prosiguen.
> ("Nocturno de los ángeles," p. 55).

or is a part of a disjointed nocturnal scene:

Soñar, soñar la noche, la calle, la escalera
y el grito de la estatua desdoblando la esquina.
> ("Nocturno de la estatua," p. 46).

In "Nocturno grito," the street expresses fragmentation, and along
it the poet searches for his own form and the sound of his voice:

Tengo miedo de mi voz
y busco mi sombra en vano.

¿Será mía aquella sombra
sin cuerpo que va pasando?
¿Y mía la voz perdida
que va la calle incendiando?

¿Qué voz, qué sombra, qué sueño
despierto que no he soñado
serán la voz y la sombra
y el sueño que me han robado? (p. 46).

The nocturnal street, along with the figure of personified night,
functions as an important motif in the representation of the dream
state of Villaurrutia's poems, and is the most important concrete
representation of this subterranean dream world.

Internal-External

Another important grouping is made up of those images which
portray or suggest both an interior and an exterior aspect. The surface and profundity of a well, the flash of reflected reality in a mirror,
the still life frozen for an instant in the frame of a picture, the subterranean psychic flow beneath the surface of conscious reality, or a
secret love hidden in the peculiar form of a fig are seemingly disparate
images which can be joined together in this way and extend across
all of the major collection.

In some of the early poems, there is a careful depiction of the
external world as well as of an internal dimension which agrees or

contrasts with states of emotion on the part of the poet. For example, in "Tarde" the sunlight and the sounds of the *estancia* are in contrast to the olfactory and visual representations of the internal world of the room, which is at that moment in agreement with the emotions of the person contemplating the scene: "Dulzura hay en el alma, y juventud, y vida". In "Remanso," the representation is reversed, with the outside world being the noise and color of the street as opposed to an internal world represented by a dark and quiet garden which in turn reflects the state of mind of the poet: "Este jardín tiene alma idéntica a la mía...".

In *Reflejos* the momentary capturing of reality in pictorial form brings about the same sense of duality. In "Soledad," for example, a personified solitude stares forth from the eyes of a woman's face painted on canvas:

> Soledad, soledad
> ¡cómo me miras desde los ojos
> de la mujer de ese cuadro!
>
> Cada día, cada día,
> todos los días...
> Cómo me miras con sus ojos hondos. (pp. 28-29).

The motif of the "marco" or picture frame is an important part of this representation of reality. The term itself is used often ("se hiela en un marco para ser espejo / y cuadro de comedor.", "Interior," p. 30), but at times a corner or a window frame will divide reality from representation:

> Deshace julio en vapor los cristales
> de las ventanas del agua y del aire.
>
> En el blanco azul tornasol del mantel
> los frutos toman posturas eternas
> para el ojo y para el pincel.
>> ("Cézanne," p. 31).

In *Nostalgia de la muerte* internal-external imagery seems to take two directions. First, as compared to external reality, the night is a hollow, echoing world in which shadowy forms move and search for some kind of meaning:

En la noche resuena, como en un mundo hueco,
el ruido de mis pasos prolongados, distantes.
Siento miedo de que no sea sino el eco
de otros pasos ajenos, que pasaron mucho antes.

("Estancias nocturnas," p. 62).

Within the confines of this world the gleaming flow of subconscious
imagery is heightened:

Y no basta cerrar los ojos en la sombra
ni hundirlos en el sueño para ya no mirar,
porque en la dura sombra y en la gruta del sueño
la misma luz nocturna nos vuelve a desvelar.

("Nocturno miedo," p. 45).

At the same time, the body and mind of the poet become a closed
world in relationship to external reality. In order to make sure that
he still lives, the poet desires to hear his own heartbeat: "¿Pondré
la oreja en mi pecho / como en el pulso la mano?" In a strange
dream, his body is killed by his own hand:

Sin gota de sangre
sin ruido ni peso
a mis pies clavados
vino a dar mi cuerpo

("Nocturno sueño," p. 49)

He still lives, however, and within the hidden caverns of his body
the bitter waters of life continue to flow:

Lo llevo en mí como un remordimiento,
pecado ajeno y sueño misterioso,
y lo arrullo y lo duermo
y lo escondo y lo cuido y le guardo el secreto.

("Nocturno mar," p. 60).

In *Canto a la primavera* the surface placidity and the hidden
anguish of a secret and unexpressed love is the motivating force of
this image system:

Te alejas de mí pensando
que me hiere tu presencia,
y no sabes que tu ausencia

> es más dolorosa cuando
> la soledad se va ahondando,
> y en el silencio sombrío,
> sin quererlo, a pesar mío,
> oigo tu voz en el eco
> y hallo tu forma en el hueco
> que has dejado en el vacío.
>
> (IV, "Décimas de nuestro amor," p. 80).

There are several important motifs which need to be considered as part of this image system. For example, the poet uses the form of the pomegranate and the fig to symbolize, in their plain exterior and intricate internal construction, the complexities of unrealized love. Love is secret, and produces sweetness in hidden chambers as does the florescence of the fig: "Amor secreto que convierte en miel la sombra, / como la florescencia en la cárcel del higo." ("Madrigal sombrío," p. 84). In the same way, the solidified blood-red sections of the pomegranate symbolize the same slow process of maturation in closed spaces:

> Si nuestro amor está hecho
> de silencios prolongados
> que nuestros labios cerrados
> maduran dentro del pecho;
> y si el corazón deshecho
> sangra como la granada
> en su sombra congelada,
> ¿por qué, dolorosa y mustia,
> no rompemos esta angustia
> para salir de la nada?
>
> (II, "Décimas de nuestro amor," p. 79).

Although the rose does not have the same intricate internalized structure as do the fig and the pomegranate, it is used by the poet to symbolize the same sense of combining superficial reality and internal profundity. The rose is usually taken as the quintessence of beauty, the poet affirms in his "Nocturno rosa," but the rose of which he is to speak is something submerged, nocturnal, immaterial, and hollow. Here the sense of internal-external is not found in a slow gathering in a closed space, but rather in the discovery of reality and beauty beneath the ordinary surface view.

A final important motif related to the development of internal-external imagery is the mirror, which appears as an important image in some twenty of Villaurrutia's compositions. Generally the word "espejo" is used in these images, but at times the surface of a well or a body of water is also seen as a mirror. The importance for the internal-external contrast can be appreciated in a composition such as "Calles" from the collection *Reflejos*:

> Caminar bajo la rendija azul,
> ¡tan alta!
> Caminar sin que los espejos
> me pongan enfrente,
> ¡tan parecido a mí!
>
> Callando, aunque el silencio
> alargue la calle endurecida.
> Caminar, sin que el eco
> grabe el oculto disco de mi voz.
>
> Al mediodía, al mediodía
> siempre, para no ir delante de mí,
> y para no seguirme
> y no andar a mis pies.
>
> De prisa, dejando atrás la compañía
> eterna, hasta quedarme solo.
> solo, sin soledad. (p. 41).

The imagery of this composition is a good deal less specific than those involving the motifs of the fig and pomegranate. The "rendija azul," the mirrors, and the silence of the streets together suggest a solitary walk through the city under a night sky, a walk which reverberates with a reflected sense of dread. The multiple "espejos" cause the poet to see himself from many angles, and although he tries to remain silent, the third stanza is almost a crying out for the brightness of midday and not the multiple reflections of the night. In the final stanza the poet presses on hurriedly, attempting to leave behind the endless repeated images of the mirrors but never quite being able to do so. In this poem, then, the internal-external relationship fragments reality endlessly into multiple glistening reflections.

An endless mirror reflection, here without the shadowy subterranean view of the previous poem, is seen in the verbal play from "Nocturno en que nada se oye":

Y en el juego angustioso de un espejo frente a otro
cae mi voz
y mi voz que madura
y mi voz quemadura
y mi bosque madura
y mi voz quema dura
como el hielo de vidrio (p. 47).

At times the reflective qualities of the mirror concentrate rather than fragment, and in this stanza from "Nocturno miedo," a wall on a deserted street becomes a pale mirror which reproduces a shadowy and solitary self:

¿Y quién entre las sombras de una calle desierta,
en el muro, lívido espejo de soledad,
no se ha visto pasar o venir a su encuentro
y no ha sentido miedo, angustia, duda mortal? (p. 45).

Corporeal

To a considerable extent, Villaurrutia uses imagery in his poems which has to do with the human body and its physical processes. In the earlier collections the body and its parts are used in a rather conventional manner as one element in a more or less organized external reality. In the later collections, however, corporeal imagery is often obsessively internal, and is used to heighten the sensorial and sensual nature of many poems. Again, several important motifs appear which need further elaboration.

The human body or form is often referred to as a statue, at times to accentuate the impossibility of recapturing experience ("Correr hacia la estatua y encontrar sólo el grito, / querer tocar el grito y sólo hallar el eco," "Nocturno de la estatua," p. 46), or to express a temporary separation of consciousness from the physical body ("en la tumba del lecho dejo mi estatua sin sangre / para salir en un momento tan lento", "Nocturno en que nada se oye," p. 47). Perhaps the best example of this motif, however, is the composition "Estatua": [3]

---

[3] "Estatua" was first published in the Mexico City literary journal *Los Sesenta* (Núm. 1, 1963), and is included in the *Obras* volume with *Canto a la primavera*.

Te has hecho unos ojos duros,
sin fondo y sin horizonte,
que no miran,
que no quieren que otros ojos
curiosos, lentos, los miren.

Te has hecho, pacientemente,
con un cuidado infinito,
un cuerpo, un cuerpo de mármol
pulido, perfecto, frío.

Y es inútil que otros ojos
pretendan tocar los tuyos
con dedos de luz,
con rayos que no ciegan
ni hacen daño.

Y es inútil que otros cuerpos
quieran mirarte de cerca
con los ojos misteriosos
que hay en la piel,
con los ojos de los dedos,
con los sensibles, despiertos,
de los labios.

Te has hecho un mundo de estatua,
lleno de ti, para ti. (p. 87).

The imagery of the poem develops an extended metaphor in which the "tú" has become as cold, as hard, and as beautiful as a marble statue. The eyes are sightless and do not return the glances of others. The body is perfectly formed and polished, but in its beauty and perfection it is completely cold and unfeeling. Stanzas 3 and 4 return again to these two sensory perceptions, and indicate that the desiring eyes of others are unable to awaken feeling and passion, and in a like manner the touch of fingers or lips is just as ineffective. The person being addressed has become deliberately (this is emphasized by the repetitions in stanzas 1, 2, and 5 of the phrase "te has hecho") a world hardened and closed in upon itself, in which emotional response is neither desired nor possible. In this poem, at least, the statue can be seen as a symbol of the impossibility of meaningful or lasting emotional relationships.

There are also several motifs which suggest the entire human form, but in reality depict only a part of it. For example, the complexity of the whole body is suggested by the tree-like shape of the nervous system:

> siento caer fuera de mí la red de mis nervios
> mas huye todo como el pez que se da cuenta
>
> ("Nocturno en que nada se oye," p. 48)

> Pero también la primavera nace
> de pronto en nuestro cuerpo,
> filtrando su inasible,
> su misteriosa savia
> en cada débil rama
> del árbol de los nervios;
>
> ("Canto a la primavera," p. 75).

A more frequent motif is that of the circulatory system of the body. Again, the whole body is suggested by the branching structure of blood vessels:

> ¡Todo!
> circula en cada rama
> del árbol de mis venas,
> acaricia mis muslos,
> inunda mis oídos,
> vive en mis ojos muertos,
> muere en mis labios duros.
>
> ("Nocturno," p. 45)

> Nocturno mar amargo
> que circula en estrechos corredores
> de corales arterias y raíces
> y venas y medusas capilares.

> Mar que teje en la sombra su tejido flotante,
> con azules agujas ensartadas
> con hilos nervios y tensos cordones.
>
> ("Nocturno mar," p. 60).

The beating of the heart and its corresponding pulse in other parts of the body are seen as indications of a very tentative and problematic existence:

¡Qué tic-tac en tu pecho
alarga la noche sin sueño!

("Noche," p. 28)

Para oír brotar la sangre
de mi corazón cerrado,
¿pondré la oreja en mi pecho
como en el pulso la mano?

Mi pecho estará vacío
y yo descorazonado
y serán mis manos duros
pulsos de mármol helado.

("Nocturno grito," p. 46).

At times the heart is the point of reference for a metaphor in which the human body is no longer the central element. For example, in "Suite del insomnio," a clock is described as follows: "¿Qué corazón avaro / cuenta el metal / de los instantes?" ("Reloj," p. 43). In "Fonógrafos," the heart becomes the whirling disk or cylinder which under the touch of the needle reveals its fixed essence of the past:

Y el corazón,
el corazón de mica
—sin diástole ni sístole—
enloquece bajo la aguja
y sangra en gritos
su pasado. (p. 36).

Other parts of the human body appear as motifs primarily in their ability to communicate sensorial perceptions. For example, eyes or the sense of sight are used less frequently than some others, but do appear occasionally as part of a sensorial reduction ("sin más que una mirada y una voz / que no recuerdan haber salido de ojos y labios", "Nocturno en que nada se oye," p. 47), or to capture a fleeting nocturnal image on the photographic plate of the retina:

Yo te dejaba ir, los ojos
cerrando, al fin te guardaba
la placa de mi retina.
¡Saldrías cercana y clara!

Por la noche revelaba
tu imagen para, de una vez, fijarla.

> Al sol, borrosa y lejana,
> ¡no era nada!
>
> ("Lugares [III]," p. 42).

The organs of speech and hearing appear much more frequently. For example, the outer ear is depicted as a labyrinthian shell ("aquí en el caracol de la oreja", "Nocturno en que nada se oye," p. 47), which has a strange fascination both because of its shape and because of its function:

> Es la rosa moldura del oído,
> la rosa oreja,
> la espiral del ruido,
> la rosa concha siempre abandonada
> en la más alta espuma de la almohada.
>
> ("Nocturno rosa," p. 58).

The inner ear or the sense of hearing is sharpened figuratively in order to catch the faint sounds of night ("El oído se aguza para ensartar un eco / lejano, o el rumor de unas voces que dejan, / al pasar, una huella de vocales perdidas.", "Nocturno," p. 53), or the infinite secret sounds of growing death:

> Mi oreja sigue su rumor secreto,
> oigo crecer sus rocas y sus plantas
> que alargan más y más sus labios dedos.
>
> ("Nocturno mar," p. 60).

The organs of speech sometimes produce sound, but in their breaking of the pervasive silence question existence and meaning:

> o cuando todo ha muerto
> tan dura y lentamente que da miedo
> alzar la voz y preguntar "quién vive"
>
> dudo si responder
> a la muda pregunta con un grito
> por temor de saber que ya no existo
>
> porque acaso la voz tampoco vive
> sino como un recuerdo en la garganta
> y no es la noche sino la ceguera
> lo que llena de sombra nuestros ojos
>
> ("Nocturno eterno," pp. 51-52).

The final sub-group of corporeal motifs is that having to do with tactile sense impressions. Most common are the hands or the fingers:

> Es la rosa del tacto en las tinieblas,
> es la rosa que avanza enardecida,
> la rosa de rosadas uñas,
> la rosa yema de los dedos ávidos,
> la rosa digital,
> la rosa ciega.
>
> ("Nocturno rosa," p. 58)

> Si tienes manos, que sean
> de un tacto sutil y blando,
> apenas sensible cuando
> anestesiado me crean;
>
> (III, "Décima muerte," p. 71).

Lips are seen not solely as organs of speech but also as organs of touch. In this stanza from "Estatua" both fingers and lips are seen metaphorically to be as productive of vivid impressions as in the sense of sight:

> Y es inútil que otros cuerpos
> quieran mirarte de cerca
> con los ojos misteriosos
> que hay en la piel,
> con los ojos de los dedos,
> con los sensibles, despiertos,
> de los labios. (p. 87).

Liquidity

Images of liquidity appear with great frequency and variety in Villaurrutia's poems. Water in multiple forms (water, rain, humidity, snow, ice) is the most important motif, and is often designated by conventional limiting names: lake, stream, river, sea, fountain, well, or pool. Other natural or manufactured fluids appear (alcohol, wine, sap, juice, honey), as also the fluids of the human body (blood, lymph, saliva, sweat). These images and motifs can be grouped in two opposing categories: those in which actual liquidity is reduced or eliminated and whose function tends to be static, and those images in which liquidity is emphasized and whose function becomes kinetic.

In the early poems the quiet waters of a lake or a well reflect a peaceful surrounding scene and the untroubled emotions of the poet:

> Y el crepúsculo rojo que a lo lejos moría
> en su último rútilo al hundirse en lo arcano
> iluminó el rostro. Yo sentí que vivía
> y la besé en la frente, y la besé en la mano.
>
> ("En la tarde que muere...," p. 3)

> El agua, que en el pozo paralizó sus ansias,
> dijo con sus cristales virtudes olvidadas,
> como nuestras abuelas en las viejas estancias,
> con los ojos abiertos y las manos cansadas.
>
> ("Bajo el sigilo de la luna," p. 21).

In *Reflejos,* static liquidity is very much a part of the "still-life" technique of many of these poems. For example, at times the entire suspended arrangement is caught in the crystal of water in a drinking glass:

> ¡Calor! Sin embargo, da pena
> beberse la "naturaleza muerta"
> que han dejado dentro del vaso.
>
> ("Cézanne," p. 31).

Frozen metaphorically for a moment, a stream becomes a broken mirror scattered through the meadow ("y el espejito roto entre la lama", "Puzzle," p. 35), and roadways become silvered streams which flow through the night:

> Arroyos que se han dormido,
> blancos de plata, se tienden
> en el verde los caminos.
>
> ("Noche," p. 37).

At times the suspended reality of water is indicative of the poet's state of mind:

> Paisaje inmóvil de cuatro colores
> en torno mío
> y en el agua.
> ¡Y yo que esperaba

hallar, en el agua siquiera,
el mismo incolor que en mi alma!

("Incolor," p. 39).

In *Nostalgia de la muerte* the night becomes at times a shadowy pool ("El que nada se oye en esta alberca de sombra", "Nocturno amor," p. 49), and the solitude of the poet a liquid shadow into which he sinks, there to find an endless bleak expanse:

Soledad, aburrimiento,
vano silencio profundo,
líquida sombra en que me hundo,
vacío del pensamiento.
Y ni siquiera el acento
de una voz indefinible
que llegue hasta el imposible
rincón de un mar infinito
a iluminar con su grito
este naufragio invisible.

("Nocturno solo," pp. 50-51).

At times the frozen hardness of ice is the result of the separation and silence felt by the poet, and fluidity and life can be restored only by heat and melting:

¿Quién medirá el espacio, quién me dirá el momento
en que se funda el hielo de mi cuerpo y consuma
el corazón inmóvil como la llama fría?

("Nocturno muerto," p. 52).

Images of liquidity in Villaurrutia's poems are often dynamic as well as static. Rivers and streams flow and reflect light, the sea ebbs and flows in tides and waves, and the blood and lymph systems of the body provide circulatory movement.

The imagery of "Arroyo," from *Reflejos,* is an example of fluidity and mobility:

¡El sol!
Hace trizas
los espejos y, hechos
azogue y vidrio,
los empuja
y los derrite.

¡Qué dulce el agua
disolviendo sales!
¡Qué fría
hirviendo siempre!
¡Cómo se astilla
contra las piedras que esculpe!
¡Cómo imanta sus agujas
rápidas!

Y cómo vence luego
el abandono
de sus crines blancas. (p. 38).

The central image of the poem is a metaphoric representation of a stream in rapid flow with the sun's rays reflecting brilliantly from its surface. In the first stanza, the light of the sun seems to break the mirror-like surface of the stream and cause it to flow, as quicksilver would move quickly across a glassy surface. The second stanza, with its series of exclamatory elements, represents the water in its onrushing flow. It is both sweet and salty, cold and boiling, fragmented and formed, and only in the third stanza is it apparent that the reality of the stream is in its rapid flow and not in its fragmented reflected images.

Another example of a dynamic image of liquidity is the composition "Mar": [4]

Te acariciaba, mar, en mi desvelo;
te soñaba en mi sueño, inesperado;
te aspiraba en la sombra recatado;
te oía en el silencio de mi duelo.

Eras, para mi cuerpo, cielo y suelo;
símbolo de mi sueño, inexplicado;
olor para mi sombra, iluminado;
rumor en el silencio de mi celo.

Te tuve ayer hirviendo entre mis manos,
caí despierto en tu profundo río,
sentí el roce de tus muslos cercanos.

---

[4] The *Obras* arrangement places this poem among the *Primeros poemas,* although it was published posthumously in 1953 and was included in *Poesía y teatro* with *Canto a la primavera.* The imagery and technique of the poem make it seem out of place among the poet's very early compositions.

Y aunque fui tuyo, entre tus brazos frío,
tu calor y tu aliento fueron vanos:
cada vez más te siento menos mío. (pp. 24-25).

The central image of the poem is a metaphor in which the sea
becomes the all in all for the poet. In the quatrains, the poet remembers in non-specific past time (the use of the imperfect tense is significant) that which the sea represented for him: dreams, aspirations,
silence, and above all symbolic sense impressions which show internal
workings of the poet's consciousness. The tercets continue the recol-
lections of the past, but here in more exact preterit. As recently as
yesterday the poet felt the warmth and profundity of the personified
ocean, and felt himself surrounded by its presence. Only in the final
line does the image touch the present, the poet feels less and less in
contact with this magnetic presence, and unable to find the union
which he desires.

The careful and extended personification in this poem suggests
strongly a symbolic interpretation. The sea might symbolize physical
love, in which the poet finds diminishing meaning, or perhaps even
poetic inspiration, which becomes progressively more difficult. The
sea could even represent the source from which all life comes, and
in this way the sonnet becomes a search for metaphysical meaning.

A more complex example of dynamic liquid imagery is provided
by the composition "Nocturno mar":

Ni tu silencio duro cristal de dura roca,
ni el frío de la mano que me tiendes,
ni tus palabras secas, sin tiempo ni color,
ni mi nombre, ni siquiera mi nombre
5   que dictas como cifra desnuda de sentido;

ni la herida profunda, ni la sangre
que mana de sus labios, palpitante,
ni la distancia cada vez más fría
sábana nieve de hospital invierno
10   tendida entre los dos como la duda;

nada, nada podrá ser más amargo
que el mar que llevo dentro, solo y ciego,
el mar antiguo edipo que me recorre a tientas
desde todos los siglos,
15   cuando mi sangre aún no era mi sangre,

cuando mi piel crecía en la piel de otro cuerpo,
cuando alguien respiraba por mí que aún no nacía.

El mar que sube mudo hasta mis labios,
el mar que se satura
20   con el mortal veneno que no mata
pues prolonga la vida y duele más que el dolor.
El mar que hace un trabajo lento y lento
forjando en la caverna de mi pecho
el puño airado de mi corazón.

25   Mar sin viento ni cielo,
sin olas, desolado,
nocturno mar sin espuma en los labios,
nocturno mar sin cólera, conforme
con lamer las paredes que lo mantienen preso
30   y esclavo que no rompe sus riberas
y ciego que no busca la luz que le robaron
y amante que no quiere sino su desamor.

Mar que arrastra despojos silenciosos,
olvidos olvidados y deseos,
35   sílabas de recuerdos y rencores,
ahogados sueños de recién nacidos,
perfiles y perfumes mutilados,
fibras de luz y náufragos cabellos.

Nocturno mar amargo
40   que circula en estrechos corredores
de corales arterias y raíces
y venas y medusas capilares.

Mar que teje en la sombra su tejido flotante,
con azules agujas ensartadas
45   con hilos nervios y tensos cordones.

Nocturno mar amargo
que humedece mi lengua con su lenta saliva,
que hace crecer mis uñas con la fuerza
de su marea oscura.

50   Mi oreja sigue su rumor secreto,
oigo crecer sus rocas y sus plantas
que alargan más y más sus labios dedos.

Lo llevo en mí como un remordimiento,
pecado ajeno y sueño misterioso,

55 y lo arrullo y lo duermo
    y lo escondo y lo cuido y le guardo el secreto. (pp. 59-60).

The central image of the poem is an extended metaphor in which
blood (life) is an internal sea in whose movements the poet senses
the bitterness and futility of his existence. The eleven stanzas of the
poem develop the image in three distinct segments. The first three
stanzas (lines 1-17) establish the basic situation from which the image
springs. The poet senses a profound separation from "tú" (silence,
cold, the aseptic whiteness of a hospital), but none of these things
can be more bitter than the secret flow which he carries within himself.
The third stanza suggests a kind of timelessness which extends backward through the aquatic fetal state to preceding generations. The
Oedipus image of line 13 conveys both a sense of groping blindness
and of inevitability.

The following six strophes (lines 18-49) become a more detailed
consideration of the bitter internal fluidity which the poet feels in
himself. In stanza 4, the sea is silent but moves slowly and surely to
the utmost extremities of the poet's being. However, its effect is not
to give life and vitality but rather to saturate with a deadly poison
and to sharpen an awareness of the painful extension of life. The
following stanza (lines 25-32) depicts this sea as being unmoved by
wind or storm, and moving in its flow along already established
courses. The following stanza (lines 33-38) indicates that the currents
and tides of this internalized sea carry with them the forgotten fragments of the poet's life, and a sense of anguish and futility is again
made apparent. Strophes 7 through 9 (lines 39-49) bring this structural section to a close by likening the movements of the bitter sea
to the circulation of blood and fluids in the human body. The process is slow and intricate (the image of weaving in lines 43-45 is
exemplary), and produces in its motions such concrete things as
fingernails.

The final two stanzas (lines 50-56) concentrate on the internali-
zation of this secret ocean. The poet is able to follow its minute
sounds, to be aware of its slow growth in which its flora and fauna
reach out grasping fingers. The poet carries all of its simplicity and
complexity within himself, at times with a sense of guilt and at other
times with a sense of mystery. As well as being aware of it, the poet

hides and cares for it as an infant, and protects the secret of its existence.

The carefully worked marine imagery of this poem again suggests a symbolic dimension. On the most elementary level the internal sea expresses the poet's awareness of and infatuation with the inner courses and chambers of the human body. In a more abstract sense the extended metaphor can represent the mysterious force of life, which flows darkly toward disenchantment and death but is nonetheless to be maintained and treasured. Life is essentially bitter to the taste, but must be lived nonetheless, pushed on by the irresistible motion of internal tides.

One final example of dynamism in the expression of liquidity is "Soneto de la granada".

The central image of the poem is the pomegranate, which has been discussed earlier as a part of internal-external imagery. Allied to this is the motif of liquidity, here with a dynamic potentiality held in abeyance. The unslaked thirst of the poet (his pain, his desire for love) is internalized and kept, in solidified segments, as the individual kernels of the fruit. There is developed, therefore, a complex metaphor which takes as its center an expression of potential liquidity: thirst (pain) = juice of pomegranate = blood. In the same way that the sections of the fruit are liquified to diminish the thirst of the person who consumes them, at some future time the solidified essence of the poet (blood, pain, thirst) will be liquified to comfort a fellow sufferer.

Again the images of the poem are very carefully worked so as to take full advantage of the expression of liquidity. The process of congealing liquidity is slow but inevitable, the sensation of thirst is constant, and future liquification and consumption is complete.

CHAPTER V

THEMES

General

The preceding chapters on language, poetic form, and imagery have in a way been preparatory to this chapter: a study of the major nuclei of meaning in Villaurrutia's poems. The earlier focus on single aspects and the use of partial explications were both appropriate and necessary, but here the major concern must be totality of poetic meaning.

Villaurrutia's poetry turns on three obsessions which find expression as the three principal themes: 1) human beings live separated one from another in inevitable and anguished solitude; 2) love, when it exists, is incomplete, secret, impossible, and at times illicit; 3) death is a constant presence in an empty and solitary existence. In the first section of this chapter, I shall examine these three thematic groupings as exemplified in a number of important poems.

In addition to the three main themes, there are several smaller complexes of meaning which will be discussed in the second part: poetry and the poetic muse, nature and the peaceful life, religious experience, and recollection of childhood.

Major Themes

Solitude

An essential awareness of separation and solitude is developed with increasing intensity in the poet's four collections. In *Primeros poemas,* for example, solitude is implied in the scenes of silent nature found in many of the poems, and anguished separation is sharply underscored in the pronominal separation of "Ellos y yo": "*Ellos* saben vivir / y reír / y besar . . . / *Yo*: sólo sé llorar . . ." (p. 7). Even the hot rays of the summer sun make visible a shadowy process of fragmentation and isolation:

> El viento, alto, en los árboles
> sonaba a río
> ¡río en el azul!
> Yo dejé ir mi corazón
> 5 al frío,
> al viento,
> al río, no sé . . .
> "Vámonos sin amor y sin deseo:
> sin dolor.
> 10 Ahora que el corazón se va
> en el frío,
> en el viento,
> en el río, vámonos . . ."
>
> La sombra, azul, aliviaba
> 15 la frente,
> ¡la frente bajo el sol!
> Yo dejé ir mi corazón
> al frío,
> a la sombra,
> 20 al azul . . .
>
> "Vámonos sin amor y sin deseo:
> sin dolor.
> Ahora que el corazón se queda
> en el frío,
> 25 en la sombra,
> en el azul, vámonos
> va-
> mo-
> nos . . ."
>
> ("Estío," pp. 15-16).

In spite of the title, which suggests the description of a brilliant summer day, the poem moves thematically in the opposite direction. In the first stanza, for example, the wind in the trees becomes a frigid stream which carries away the heart (the consciousness?) of the poet. The second stanza, set off by quotation marks as if it were spoken to another person (perhaps even to the speaker himself), repeats in more uneven metrical terms some of the same elments, and with a first person plural command form recommends emotionless movement in the same stream. The third stanza, equally uneven from a metrical point of view, underscores with many of the same elements the shadowy movement away from the rays of the sun. The final stanza, again with quotation marks, represents the heart and being of the poet in the precise moment of surrender to the shadowy flow. Here the verb "quedarse" is used in place of "irse", and the command form is repeated with a final fragmentation. Thus the poet moves away from the brilliance of the external world lighted by sunshine into the somber, and in a way comforting, depths of contemplative solitude.

In *Reflejos,* the theme is considerably expanded and runs the gamut from objective to subjective treatment. For example, the description of the solitude and isolation of a small Mexican town has little to do with the psychic reality of the poet:

> Aquel pueblo se quedó soltero,
> conforme con su iglesia,
> embozado en su silencio,
> bajo la paja —oro, mediodía—
> de su sombrero ancho,
> sin nada más:
> en las fichas del cementerio
> los + son —.
>
> Aquel pueblo cerró los ojos
> para no ver la cinta de cielo
> que se lleva el río,
> y la carrera de los rieles
> delante del tren.
> El cielo y el agua,
> la vía, la vía
> —vidas paralelas—,
> piensan, ¡ay! encontrarse
> en la ciudad.
>
> Se le fue la gente
> con todo y ganado.
> Se le fue la luna novia,
> ¡la noche le dice
> que allá en la ciudad

se ha casado!
Le dejaron, vacías, las casas
¡a él que no sabe jugar
a los dados!

("Pueblo," pp. 34-35).

A personification of the town is the central device for carrying out the theme of isolation. In the first stanza, for example, it is represented as remaining in perpetual bachelorhood, sleeping in the golden silence between the church and the cemetery. Perhaps the most Mexican detail, and one of the few in all of Villaurrutia's verses, is the broadbrimmed Mexican hat (perhaps suggested by the rays of the midday sun) under which the personified town finds shade and protection. In the second strophe the person-town closes his eyes so as not to see those pathways which lead away from isolation. The river against the sky and the parallel rails of the railroad right-of-way suggest a coming together only at some distant point, here suggested as the city. The personification continues into the third stanza as well, and the town becomes a lonely person who has been deserted by all others and has been left to gaze aimlessly at the empty shapes around him. The city has attracted the inhabitants of the town, and even the moon is a girl who has left to find marriage in the city. The empty houses are like parts of a pointless game of dice, a figure which is important both as a part of the visual representation of the poem and for the thematic development of solitude.

In "Cinematógrafo," the poet wanders along a lonely street which takes on the elongated shape and darkness of a movie theater:

En la calle, la plancha gris del cielo,
más baja cada vez,
nos empareda vivos . . .
El corazón, sin frío de invierno,
quiere llorar su juventud
a oscuras.

En este túnel el hollín
unta las caras,
y sólo así mi corazón se atreve.

En este túnel sopla
la música delgada,
y es tan largo que tardaré en salir

por aquella puerta con luz
donde lloran dos hombres
que quisieran estar a oscuras.

¿Por qué no pagarán la entrada? (p. 41).

The first stanza establishes the visual limits of the scene. The street is darkened and oppressed by the heavy grayness of the night sky, and the absence of wintry cold suggested in line 4 releases emotions rather than inhibiting them. In the short second stanza the walled-in street is a tunnel in which faces are blackened by the shadows and the anonymity necessary for a release of emotions is maintained. The longer third stanza continues the same figure, but now music is heard as if in a movie house and an illuminated exit (the lighted door of the theater?) is made a part of the description. The reference to the two men who stand crying at the door is a puzzling one. It is possible to see them as two people who have not paid for a ticket into the theater, and therefore must remain outside (this would also explain in part the final line of the poem). Perhaps they have even been inside the theater and have been moved to emotion by what they have seen. However, if the tunnel of the poem is really a street which has many of the characteristics of a movie theater, then the two men would have to be seen as being unwilling or unable to enter the dark solitude of the street, perhaps without the power to pay the emotional price necessary. At any rate, the poet sees himself as separated by considerable distance from those two figures and shrouded in the blackening which is provided by the scene which he develops.

In "Soledad," the poet gazes at a painting and sees his feeling of solitude reflected in the eyes of one of the figures:

Soledad, soledad
!cómo me miras desde los ojos
de la mujer de ese cuadro!

Cada día, cada día,
todos los días . . .
Cómo me miras con sus ojos hondos.

Si me quejo, parece que sus ojos
me quisieran decir que no estoy solo.

> Y cuando espero lo que nunca llega,
> me quisieran decir: aquí me tienes.
>
> Y cuando lloro —algunas veces lloro—
> también sus ojos se humedecen,
> o será que los miro con los míos. (pp. 28-29).

Solitude is personified through the development of the poem, and is the presence which gives some kind of life to the figure in the painting. The first two stanzas, for example, develop this basic distinction by careful use of second and third person forms, particularly in line 6. The final three stanzas represent a contradictory view of the theme based on that duality already established. The eyes of the painting seem to tell him that he is not alone, but the only presence which accompanies him is that of the personified figure of solitude speaking through those eyes. They also seem to be wet with tears, but as the poet observes, this is probably due to his own tears, which come perhaps from the realization of an inescapable solitude which follows his every motion.

The most internalized treatment of the theme is found in "Amplificaciones," in which candlelight throws flickering shadows on the wall and the poet looks within himself for some kind of meaning:

> En el cuarto del pueblo,
> fantástico y desnudo,
> amarillo de luz de vela,
> sobrecogido,
> mis sienes dan la hora
> en no sé qué reloj
> puntual y eterno.
>
> La soledad se agranda
> como las sombras
> en la sábana del muro,
> como las caras de ayer
> asomadas para adentro
> en el marco de sus ventanas.
>
> Y el silencio se mueve
> y vibra
> en torno de la llama blanda,
> como el ala —¿de qué presagio?,
> ¿de qué insecto?— que acaricia,
> que enfría, que empequeñece. (pp. 36-37).

The first stanza develops the basic figure of the poem, a room in which the world is reduced to two things: the sputtering yellow light of a candle and the inexorable temporal flow of the poet's life as seen in the pulse of his temples. In the second stanza solitude is represented in two similes which are interconnected by the flickering light of the candle. Solitude resembles, the poet says, the moving shadows which are thrown on the whiteness of the wall or the remembered faces of yesterday which are captured within the frame of a window. In another extended simile, the third strophe develops silence as something which is visible and circles the flame of the candle as if it were a moth attracted by its light. This silence caresses but at the same time reduces the size of things and creates a sensation of coldness. Through the careful imagery of the poem, the poet turns his awareness inward and finds there the hazy figures of solitude and silence.

In *Nostalgia de la muerte* the descriptive aspect of the theme disappears and solitude becomes limitless and internalized. Perhaps the best example of this view of solitude is "Nocturno en que nada se oye," in which the consciousness of the poet descends into an endless aquatic world:

```
    En medio de un silencio desierto como la calle antes del crimen
    sin respirar siquiera para que nada turbe mi muerte
    en esta soledad sin paredes
    al tiempo que huyeron los ángulos
 5  en la tumba del lecho dejo mi estatua sin sangre
    para salir en un momento tan lento
    en un interminable descenso
    sin brazos que tender
    sin dedos para alcanzar la escala que cae de un piano invisible
10  sin más que una mirada y una voz
    que no recuerdan haber salido de ojos y labios
    ¿qué son labios? ¿qué son miradas que son labios?
    y mi voz ya no es mía
    dentro del agua que no moja
15  dentro del aire de vidrio
    dentro del fuego lívido que corta como el grito
    Y en el juego angustioso de un espejo frente a otro
    cae mi voz
    y mi voz que madura
20  y mi voz quemadura
    y mi bosque madura
    y mi voz quema dura
```

```
     como el hielo de vidrio
     como el grito de hielo
25   aquí en el caracol de la oreja
     el latido de un mar en el que no sé nada
     en el que no se nada
     porque he dejado pies y brazos en la orilla
     siento caer fuera de mí la red de mis nervios
30   mas huye todo como el pez que se da cuenta
     hasta siento en el pulso de mis sienes
     muda telegrafía a la que nadie responde
     porque el sueño y la muerte nada tienen ya que decirse.
```

(pp. 47-48).

From the point of view of metrics and structure, this is one of the poems which comes closest to the reproduction of a free-flowing mental stream. There are no stanzas, the line lengths vary widely and have no particular pattern, and there is only scattered assonance. Even the punctuation is greatly reduced, and the impression of continuous movement from one line to another is enhanced. Nevertheless, it is possible to divide the poem into four structural elements which are in keeping with the thematic development as well.

The first of these divisions includes the first twelve lines of the poem, in which the general thematic lines of the poem are established. The silence and solitude are limitless (lines 1-4), and in a death-like descent the consciousness of the poet leaves behind the totality of his physical body. The descent is momentary, but at the same time interminable, and the poet retains only the powers of sight and speech. As the descent becomes deeper (lines 8-12) this reduction becomes more pronounced but also is expressed more chaotically (the interrogative utterances of line 12 are exemplary of this pattern).

The second segment is made up of lines 13-16, in which the descent into solitude has become so deep that the poet's voice no longer belongs to him, and certain elemental relationships no longer operate: water does not make things wet, air is as hard and brilliant as glass, and livid fire cuts and penetrates only as a remembered shout.

The third element is made up of lines 17-24, and continues the representation of deepened dream-like solitude. The series of reflecting mirrors which produces the endless echoing and changing of the poet's voice is an anguished and sterile reverberation which is finally expressed in the intense thermic contrasts of heat and ice (lines 22-24).

In the final segment (lines 25-33), the state of solitude is represented as a profound sea in which the poet is unable to swim or move himself. This is the moment of deepest descent, and the poet feels that even the impulses of his nervous and circulatory systems fall into silence. The verbal plays of this last segment emphasize strongly the difficulty or impossibility of communication of any sort, and the silence and anguished solitude of the dream foreshadow the immobility and the muteness of death.

The same sense of anguished separation and silence is expressed strongly in the five compositions grouped under the title "Estancias nocturnas":

Sonámbulo, dormido y despierto a la vez,
en silencio recorro la ciudad sumergida.
¡Y dudo! Y no me atrevo a preguntarme si es
el despertar de un sueño o es un sueño mi vida.

En la noche resuena, como en un mundo hueco,
el ruido de mis pasos prolongados, distantes.
Siento miedo de que no sea sino el eco
de otros pasos ajenos, que pasaron mucho antes.

Miedo de no ser nada más que un jirón del sueño
de alguien —¿de Dios?— que sueña en este mundo amargo.
Miedo de que despierte ese alguien —¿Dios?—, el dueño
de un sueño cada vez más profundo y más largo.

Estrella que te asomas, temblorosa y despierta,
tímida aparición en el cielo impasible,
tú, como yo —hace siglos—, estás helada y muerta,
mas por tu propia luz sigues siendo visible.

¡Seré polvo en el polvo y olvido en el olvido!
Pero alguien, en la angustia de una noche vacía,
sin saberlo él, ni yo, alguien que no ha nacido
dirá con mis palabras su nocturna agonía. (pp. 62-63).

The *estancias* are careful quatrain stanzas using Alexanderine lines and a constant ABAB rhyme scheme. The only metrical complication is that of a frequent series of run-on lines which alter somewhat the measured flow of the conventional metrics. In spite of an evident desire on the part of the poet (or the editors of the edition) to separate into five distinct compositions, the *estancias* should be read as a single poem on the meaning of existence from the point of view of anguished solitude. If seen in that fashion, there are three divisions which need to be considered. The first *estancia* sets the scene, in which the poet wanders in silence through a dream-like city. It is against that background that the persistent question comes as to dream or reality, meaning or lack of meaning. *Estancias* 2 and 3 form a second structural element in the poem. The poet hears his own footsteps resounding in the hollow world of the city, and fears that they are but the echo of other footsteps from times past. This fear carries him to the more profound concern that perhaps his entire existence is nothing more than the dream of someone else, perhaps of God himself, who has powers superior to his own. *Estancias* 4 and 5 make up the final structural element of the poem. The poet raises his eyes to the night sky and likens himself to the early star that he sees there; he, as the star, is able to give an impression of life and light in spite of the reality of coldness and death. In the same way that the star expresses to him both existence and death, his words will help some person as yet unborn to express the same kind of anguish.

Along the deserted streets of a phantasmal world the solitary figure of the poet searches for himself and some kind of meaning:

> Tengo miedo de mi voz
> y busco mi sombra en vano.
>
> ¿Será mía aquella sombra
> sin cuerpo que va pasando?
> ¿Y mía la voz perdida
> que va la calle incendiando?
>
> ¿Qué voz, qué sombra, qué sueño
> despierto que no he soñado
> serán la voz y la sombra
> y el sueño que me han robado?
>
> Para oír brotar la sangre
> de mi corazón cerrado,
> ¿pondré la oreja en mi pecho
> como en el pulso la mano?
>
> Mi pecho estará vacío
> y yo descorazonado
> y serán mis manos duros
> pulsos de mármol helado.
>
> ("Nocturno grito," p. 46).

The poem is presented in octosyllabic quatrains with conventional rhyme scheme. The only variation from that pattern is the unrhymed couplet which serves as the first stanza. The theme is isolation and an internalized searching for meaning, and is developed in three segments. The first is the two-line introductory stanza which presents the poet's sense of fear and his search for shadowy form. This is an ambiguous search, and it is interesting to note that these two lines are the only declarative elements in the whole poem. The second structural element is made up of the following two stanzas. Three interrogations built on verbs in the future of probability underscore sharply the tentativeness of the inquiry by the poet as to the identity of the formless shadow and the lost voice which move along the street. These have been stolen from the poet, and identification is now probably impossible. The third structural segment of the poem is made up of the final two stanzas. The poet turns to an examination of himself, but one which is almost as tentative as the questions about his disembodied shadow and voice. In order to be sure that his heart is beating, it is necessary for the poet to put figuratively his ear to his own chest as he would his hand on the pulse in his wrist. In so doing, the poet will undoubtedly find that he is but an empty shell and as cold as marble (one should note the poet's pun on "descorazonado", with a double meaning as "disheartened" and "de-hearted"). Here again the direction of the poem is from a background of silence and isolation toward emptiness and death.

At times the search for self and meaning in anguished isolation reaches frenetic proportions, as can be seen in "Nocturno de la estatua":

> Soñar, soñar la noche, la calle, la escalera
> y el grito de la estatua desdoblando la esquina.
>
> Correr hacia la estatua y encontrar sólo el grito,
> querer tocar el grito y sólo hallar el eco,
> querer asir el eco y encontrar sólo el muro
> y correr hacia el muro y tocar un espejo.
> Hallar en el espejo la estatua asesinada,
> sacarla de la sangre de su sombra,
> vestirla en un cerrar de ojos,
> acariciarla como a una hermana imprevista
> y jugar con las fichas de sus dedos
> y contar a su oreja cien veces cien cien veces
> hasta oírla decir: "estoy muerta de sueño." (pp. 46-47).

The poem is structured in two stanzas of unequal length. The first of these is an unrhymed couplet which presents the thematic problem of the poem: the dream of the night street and of the statue, another shadowy human figure. These elements are represented as if in a dream, without precise time or person. The second and longer stanza continues the same imprecision, as well as making use of the elements already introduced in the brief beginning stanza. There is a sense of constant movement in pursuit of the shadowy figure of the statue, a movement which is rewarded only by partial perception. First the statue, then the scream, then the echo, then the wall, and finally the mirror are illusive, and escape the grasp of the pursuer. Only in the mirror can the form of the statue finally be touched, and here only because of violent death. The successively connected images, the careful impersonality and nontemporality of the tenses, and the feverish, almost insane, movement of the poem all seem to suggest a symbolic search for self along the deserted streets of the subconscious, a search which ends, as most of the other poems using the same theme, in incompleteness and death.

The theme of solitude does not figure strongly in *Canto a la primavera,* but there is one late poem which shows that the theme was not entirely forgotten. The short poem "Volver...," which in spite of its placement in the second edition of Villaurrutia's works was probably one of the poet's last compositions,[1] is a consideration in rather contemplative terms of the state of solitude which had been one of the essences of the poet's existence:

> Volver a una patria lejana,
> volver a una patria olvidada,
> oscuramente deformada
> por el destierro en esta tierra.
> ¡Salir del aire que me encierra!
> Y anclar otra vez en la nada.
> La noche es mi madre y mi hermana,
> la nada es mi patria lejana,
> la nada llena de silencio,
> la nada llena de vacío,

---

[1] This composition was found in the poet's coat pocket at the time of his death, but was not published until 1960 when it appeared in *Cuadernos de Bellas Artes,* Núm. 5 (dic. de 1960). For some reason the editors of the second edition chose to include this poem with *Nostalgia de la muerte.*

la nada sin tiempo ni frío,
la nada en que no pasa nada. (pp. 69-70).

"La nada," empty, silent, inactive, and dark, is represented as
the distant homeland toward which the poet desires to travel, leaving
behind the elements and distortions of life on earth. The poem is a
fitting climax to the development of this particular theme. Gone are
the frantic and anguished wanderings of the earlier poems, and
only the desire for silence and solitude remains, a desire purified and
refined by the fires of previous emotions. The poet no longer seems
to dread but rather to be resigned and even desirous of such a state.

Love

This theme appears abundantly in all of the collections of the
poet, though perhaps more importantly in the early poems with a
somewhat conventional turn and in the last collection with a strong
sense of anguish and unfulfillment. Some examples from the various
collections will make these distinctions and developments clear.

In *Primeros poemas* love is usually represented in positive emotional terms with just a suggestion of bitterness or uncertainty. "Canción apasionada" is an appropriate example:

> Como la primavera, ponía
> en cada espíritu un azoro;
> en su sonrisa desleía
> la miel del ansia que encendía
> en un relámpago sonoro.
>
> Y como la noche, callaba,
> y en el silencio azul y fuerte
> de sus pupilas, concentraba
> un temblor mayor que la muerte...
>
> Su voz era mansa y cercana;
> tenía brillos de manzana.
> Y mi fervor asiduo ardía
> en su carne como una llama
> que ningún soplo inclinaría.
>
> ¡Qué fiel el zumo que su boca
> exprimió en la mía temblorosa!
> Su calor en mi alma coloca
> reminiscente y roja rosa.

> ¡Qué firme apego el de sus brazos!
> Lo siente ahora el desamor
> en que se inundan mis ribazos
> y en que se calla mi clamor ... (p. 17).

The poem is presented in careful eneasyllabic lines with a simple ABAB scheme of consonantal rhyme. The two stanzas which depart from the quatrain pattern vary the system somewhat, but in general the impression is one of order and control.

The theme of remembered love is developed lineally along the five stanzas of the poem. The first three depend on a series of interconnected descriptive similes comparing the remembered figure of the beloved to spring, night, and the polished brilliance of an apple. The poet's emotion is also compared to a flame which cannot be extinguished or even moved from its position. The last two stanzas begin with exclamatory utterances and with a more contemplative idea. In stanza 4 the poet remembers the touch of his beloved and the warmth which that presence, or even remembered presence, leaves with him. In stanza 5 an embrace is recalled, and the final three lines contrast the bitter present to the remembered passions of the past. The lack of love at the present moment overflows all and silences the poet's bitter outcries. This poem characterizes, then, the early development of the theme: remembered emotion contrasted with an unfulfilled present.

The composition "Más que lento," is which the experience of love is the present and unfulfilled desire of the past, is a contrasting example:

> Ya se alivia el alma mía
> trémula y amarilla;
> y recibe la unción apasionada
> de tu mano ... Y la fría
> rigidez de mi frente,
> dulcemente entibiada,
> ya se siente ...
>
> Yo no sé si mi mal indefinido
> se decolora o se desviste,
> pero ya no hace ruido.
>
> Yo no sé si la luz que todo anega,
> o el latido leal que te apresura

en mis sienes, o el ansia prematura,
inunda las pupilas y las ciega.

Qué conmovida está mi boca,
e inconforme.
Y distinto mi cuerpo
a la distinta llama de tu sangre.
Y mi sed ulterior acaso es poca.

Siento una languidez, y un desvaído
cansancio, casi de relato
pueril... Me siento como
en el claroscuro envejecido
de un melancólico retrato... (pp. 23-24).

Here the metrical form of the poem is a good deal less regular than
is the composition just discussed. Line lengths vary widely in some
of the strophes, consonantal rhyme exists but with less of an impression of established scheme, and the patterns of the strophe range
from seven to three lines in length. The development of the theme,
also, seems to be less linear, and can be divided into four segments.
The first of these is the first stanza of the poem, in which the basic
relationships are established. The soul of the poet receives the comforting touch of his beloved's hand, and the hardness and cold of
his being are reduced. The adjective "amarilla" suggest, however, that
the soul's jaundice is not entirely removed. The second segment is
made up of the two following stanzas, which begin with a parallel
negative declaration. The warmth of the present is recognized, but
the discoloration and the anxieties are reduced only for the moment. The strong present emotion obstructs or blinds temporarily,
and without doubt the past state will return again. The fourth stanza,
with its suggestion of exclamation, constitutes the third segment of
the poem. Again certain corporeal elements of the poet's being (mouth,
body, blood) recognize the distinctness of the present moment, but
at the same time the thirst of the past is only reduced, not entirely
removed. The final stanza forms the fourth thematic segment of the
poem, and though the present view is maintained the impression is
one of tiredness and flaccidity rather than joy and passion. Instead of
feeling the joy of fulfillment which might be expected from the experience of the present moment, the poet feels that his past weighs
as heavily upon him as if he were a figure in the faded colors of an

old painting. In this poem, then, present love is expressed, but with a strong coloration of melancholy from the past.

The theme of love appears less frequently in *Reflejos* and *Nostalgia de la muerte,* but there are nonetheless several poems from those two collections that should be considered. For example, the composition "Noche" from *Reflejos* is a typically sensorial representation of a present intimate moment of sexual love, in which boredom and pain are also to be found:

> ¡Qué tic-tac en tu pecho
> alarga la noche sin sueño!
>
> La media sombra viste,
> móvil, nuestros cuerpos desnudos
> y ya les da brillos de finas maderas
> o, avara, los confunde opacos.
>
> —Gocemos, si quieres,
> provocando el segundo de muerte
> para luego caer —¿en qué cansancio?,
> ¿en qué dolor?— como en un pozo
> sin fin de luz de aurora . . .
>
> Callemos en la noche última;
> aguardemos sin despedida;
> este polvo blanco
> —de luna ¡claro!—
> nos vuelve románticos. (p. 28).

The first two stanzas of this poem develop in sensorial terms the main point of the poem: the night is measured in the endless ticking of the beloved's heart, and the darkness of the night gives a contradictory sense of mobility and of carefully sculptured beauty to the nude bodies of the lovers. The third stanza deals with the sensations of love itself, first as a moment of death-like orgasm and then as a contrary all-consuming *ennui* and even pain. In the fourth stanza there is no need to speak; the lovers know well all of the limits of this experience and live it as if it were their last night together. The handling of the theme here is much more frankly sensual than in the previous poems, but continues the same bitter-sweet quality which has already been commented on. Love exists and can be experienced, but is essentially physical and inevitably transitory.

In *Nostalgia de la muerte* there are two compositions which should be commented on in this discussion of the theme of love. The first is the rather long "Nocturno amor":

El que nada se oye en esta alberca de sombra
no sé cómo mis brazos no se hieren
en tu respiración sigo la angustia del crimen
y caes en la red que tiende el sueño
5 Guardas el nombre de tu cómplice en los ojos
pero encuentro tus párpados más duros que el silencio
y antes que compartirlo matarías el goce
de entregarte en el sueño con los ojos cerrados
sufro al sentir la dicha con que tu cuerpo busca
10 el cuerpo que te vence más que el sueño
y comparo la fiebre de tus manos
con mis manos de hielo
y el temblor de tus sienes con mi pulso perdido
y el yeso de mis muslos con la piel de los tuyos
15 que la sombra corroe con su lepra incurable
Ya sé cuál es el sexo de tu boca
y lo que guarda la avaricia de tu axila
y maldigo el rumor que inunda el laberinto de tu oreja
sobre la almohada de espuma
20 sobre la dura página de nieve
No la sangre que huyó de mí como del arco huye la flecha
sino la cólera circula por mis arterias
amarilla de incendio en mitad de la noche
y todas las palabras en la prisión de la boca
25 y una sed que en el agua del espejo
sacia su sed con una sed idéntica
De qué noche despierto a esta desnuda
noche larga y cruel noche que ya no es noche
junto a tu cuerpo más muerto que muerto
30 que no es tu cuerpo ya sino su hueco
porque la ausencia de tu sueño ha matado a la muerte
y es tan grande mi frío que con un calor nuevo
abre mis ojos donde la sombra es más dura
y más clara y más luz que la luz misma
35 y resucita en mí lo que no ha sido
y es un dolor inesperado y aún más frío y más fuego
no ser sino la estatua que despierta
en la alcoba de un mundo en el que todo ha muerto.

(pp. 49-50).

Here again, as was the case with "Nocturno en que nada se oye," there is an evident attempt to approximate incoherent mental flow. There is almost no punctuation, no stanza divisions at all, line length varies widely and with no pattern, and while there is some scattered assonance, there is no system of end rhyme. In addition, there is an overriding sense of disconnection between contiguous grammatical elements of the poem, and it is difficult to suggest any lineal development.

As the title suggests, the poem has to do with the theme of love and the principal vehicle is a *yo — tú* relationship. As developed throughout the poem, however, it is not a relationship of passionate fulfillment but rather the opposite: a secretive, jealous love which finds expression in emptiness and death.

Although the poet marks no stanza at all, it is possible to separate the poem into five structural segments. The first of these (lines 1-4) presents the basic elements of the poem: a shadowy dreamstate, the presence of both *yo* and *tú*, and the sense of wrong-doing. A characteristic non-sequentiality is also seen clearly; none of the lines is related grammatically or conceptually to the contiguous ones but instead each line stands alone as a separate figure. The second segment (lines 5-15) develops several of these basic ideas further. The *yo — tú* relationship is continued, with the *yo* very much awake in the world of dreams and the *tú* asleep and therefore incommunicative. The sense of something criminal is reflected in several of the words ("cómplice," "matarías"), but the beloved person continues to sleep and the poet finds no response to his jealous searchings. The differences between the two people are striking and serve as the final element in this segment: heat versus cold, obvious indication of heartbeat and circulation versus imperceptible pulse, the softness of the beloved's skin as opposed to the hardness ("yeso") of that of the poet. Lines 16-20 form the third structural element of the poem, and intensify the corporeal sensuality with which the poet regards his beloved. He looks upon various parts of the body as having almost a life or passion of their own, and again feels jealousy for even those involuntary processes which are beyond his control. The fourth element is formed by lines 21-26, in which the poet, almost as in a nightmare, is consumed by an intense anger as if it were the life-giving substance which circulates through his body. The images of light, sound, and reflection all support this anguished circulation. The final segment (lines 27-38) is the longest of the five, and probably the most complex. The continued silence of the beloved, submerged in the pleasures of a distant dream, has deepened the sense of anguish on the part of the poet and caused him to see everything around him as cold and dead, even the body of the beloved person which is near to him. The deep frigidness which the poet feels is so intense that it is perceived at times with a contradictory sense of heat and light, a sensation which only intensifies the feeling of isolation and death which consumes him. With intense pain, represented in these contradictory terms, the poet sees himself as a petrified figure ("estatua") who struggles to uncertain wakefulness surrounded only by death.

Another important example of this theme in *Nostalgia de la muerte* is "Nocturno de los ángeles":

Se diría que las calles fluyen dulcemente en la noche.
Las luces no son tan vivas que logren desvelar el secreto,
el secreto que los hombres que van y vienen conocen,
porque todos están en el secreto
5   y nada se ganaría con partirlo en mil pedazos
si, por el contrario, es tan dulce guardarlo
y compartirlo sólo con la persona elegida.

Si cada uno dijera en un momento dado,
en sólo una palabra, lo que piensa,
10 las cinco letras del DESEO formarían una enorme cicatriz
        luminosa,
una constelación más antigua, más viva aún que las otras.
Y esa constelación sería como un ardiente sexo
en el profundo cuerpo de la noche,
o, mejor, como los Gemelos que por vez primera en la vida
15 se miraran de frente, a los ojos, y se abrazaran ya para
        siempre.

De pronto el río de la calle se puebla de sedientos seres,
caminan, se detienen, prosiguen.
Cambian miradas, atreven sonrisas
forman imprevistas parejas . . .

20 Hay recodos y bancos de sombra,
orillas de indefinibles formas profundas
y súbitos huecos de luz que ciega
y puertas que ceden a la presión más leve.

El río de la calle queda desierto un instante.
25 Luego parece remontar de sí mismo
deseoso de volver a empezar.
Queda un momento paralizado, mudo, anhelante
como el corazón entre dos espasmos.

Pero una nueva pulsación, un nuevo latido
30   arroja al río de la calle nuevos sedientos seres.
Se cruzan, se entrecruzan y suben.
Vuelan a ras de tierra.
Nadan de pie, tan milagrosamente
que nadie se atrevería a decir que no caminan.

35   ¡Son los ángeles!
Han bajado a la tierra
por invisibles escalas.
Vienen del mar, que es el espejo del cielo,
en barcos de humo y sombra,
40   a fundirse y confundirse con los mortales,
a rendir sus frentes en los muslos de las mujeres,
a dejar que otras manos palpen sus cuerpos febrilmente,
y que otros cuerpos busquen los suyos hasta encontrarlos
como se encuentran al cerrarse los labios de una misma boca,
45   a fatigar su boca tanto tiempo inactiva,
a poner en libertad sus lenguas de fuego,
a decir las canciones, los juramentos, las malas palabras
en que los hombres concentran el antiguo misterio
de la carne, la sangre y el deseo.

50   Tienen nombres supuestos, divinamente sencillos.
Se llaman Dick o John, o Marvin o Louis.
En nada sino en la belleza se distinguen de los mortales.
Caminan, se detienen, prosiguen.
Cambian miradas, atreven sonrisas.
55   Forman imprevistas parejas.

Sonríen maliciosamente al subir en los ascensores de los hoteles
donde aún se practica el vuelo lento y vertical.
En sus cuerpos desnudos hay huellas celestiales;
signos, estrellas y letras azules.
60   Se dejan caer en las camas, se hunden en las almohadas
que los hacen pensar todavía un momento en las nubes.
Pero cierran los ojos para entregarse mejor a los goces de su
        encarnación misteriosa,
y, cuando duermen, sueñan no con los ángeles sino con los
        mortales.

                              Los Angeles, California. (pp. 55-57).

Tomás Segovia finds this poem to be unique among the *nocturnos*
in that it is, as he puts it, "un poco sonriente." [2] The poet's obvious

---

    [2] "Xavier Villaurrutia," *Revista Mexicana de Literatura*, Núm. 16-18
(oct.-dic. de 1960), 60.

pun on the name of the city of Los Angeles (the poem was at least conceived during the time that Villaurrutia was traveling and studying in the United States) might lead one to agree in part with that opinion, though for me the tone is not one of levity. This is a poem on homosexual love, incomplete, unrealized, and represented in terms of physical desire.

Though the poet divides the composition into stanzas, there is no fixed length or arrangement for those divisions. Line length varies very widely and again with no visible patterning, and aside from scattered assonance there is no rhyme at all. The development of the theme is built on the contrast "ángeles — mortales" and the ten stanzas of the poem can be divided into three developmental segments.

The first of these elements (lines 1-15) develops the setting for the entire poem and also the first element of the contrast. The scene is a nocturnal one, in which the streets seem to flow as rivers and people on them move as silent shadows. The attention seems focused here on "mortales" or "hombres", though beneath the surface of each man lies a secret desire which is revealed only during the night. The use of sexual imagery in the second stanza underlines sharply an element of physical sensuality which persists throughout the poem. The second segment (lines 16-34) depicts, on the flowing rivers of nocturnal streets, the movement of two series of "sedientos seres" who walk about, gaze at each other, form couples, and then enter suddenly into lighted doors which open up along the street. These beings are obviously not mortals as were those described in the previous stanzas, but often transport themselves as if they were flying or even swimming in a standing position.

The final structural segment of the poem (lines 35-64) begins by affirming that these mysterious figurations are "los ángeles", who have come to the earth to find some sort of relationship with mortals. They come from the sea, as some kind of mysterious seafarers,[3] and in the same way that the sky finds its reflection in the sea these beings have come to reflect and release with tongues of fire the expression of the sensuality and desire which lies immediately beneath the surface of mortal beings. Again, the imagery is highly sexual, and

---

[3] It is interesting to note that in the autographed manuscript of the poem there are a number of characteristic line drawings by the poet which indicate that at one point at least he conceived of these figures as sailors dressed in traditional mariners' garb.

physical desire is represented strongly in repeated tactile sense impressions. They are more beautiful than the mortal beings with whom they desire to associate, and although they carry celestial markings on their bodies (perhaps a reference to a sailor's tattoo?) they have taken on mortal form and when they sleep dream not of angels but of mortals.

The final meaning of this very complex poem depends on the successful interpretation of the "ángeles — mortales" contrast. On a most elementary level, it is possible to see the mortals as the usual inhabitants of a port city, and the angels to be strangers who mingle with them, as sailors on liberty from their assignments. However, the highly sensual imagery and the nocturnal backdrop for the poem makes this interpretation hardly satisfactory. A better approach is to suggest that the contrast is symbolic of a dual expression of desire. The mortal, or conscious, represses a somewhat secret and shameful awareness of this desire, and only in the completely unfettered existence of the angels does all that which is hidden and repressed find expression. Every man, this interpretation would suggest, has both aspects in his personality, and only in the shadowy galleries of the night can his repressed desires be expressed. A third interpretation is to see the "ángeles — mortales" contrast as representing homosexual love and desire. The poet makes use of a mythical — astronomical reference to the Twins to suggest an all-consuming emotion. Mortals and angels have the same form, but nonetheless desire each other and can find expression for this desire only in the mysterious coupling which is possible in the limitless shadows of the night.

In *Canto a la primavera* the theme of love is primary, and can be found in almost every composition in the entire collection. Here again the emotional response depicted is not one of joy and fulfillment, but rather of incompleteness and despair.

"Décimas de nuestro amor," is probably the most imposing and carefully organized expression of the theme. This composition is made up of ten carefully worked *décimas* which develop the opposing multiple facets of an anguished and unrealized love.

The first *décima* serves as a prologue to those that follow:

I

A mí mismo me prohibo
revelar nuestro secreto,

decir tu nombre completo
o escribirlo cuando escribo.
Prisionero de ti, vivo
buscándote en la sombría
caverna de mi agonía.
Y cuando a solas te invoco,
en la oscura piedra toco
tu impasible compañía. (p. 79).

In this *décima* the essential qualities of the entire poem are presented. The central relationship is that of a *yo* who is present and in a state of anguish and a *tú* who is distant and indifferent. The search for love does not exist face to face with the beloved person, but rather in the hidden and darkened caverns of the lover's own consciousness. It is here that he realizes that their relationship is secret and even prohibited, and that the beloved exists only as an impassive, indifferent presence.

The following two *décimas* make up the second thematic segment of the poem:

II

Si nuestro amor está hecho
de silencios prolongados
que nuestros labios cerrados
maduran dentro del pecho;
y si el corazón deshecho
sangra como la granada
en su sombra congelada,
¿por qué, dolorosa y mustia,
no rompemos esta angustia
para salir de la nada?

III

Por el temor de quererme
tanto como yo te quiero,
has preferido, primero,
para salvarte, perderme.
Pero está mudo e inerme
tu corazón, de tal suerte
que si no me dejas verte
es por no ver en la mía
la imagen de tu agonía:
porque mi muerte es tu muerte. (p. 79).

These two stanzas pursue further the essence of hidden love, and represent two of its aspects. This love is unexpressed and imprisoned, as the figure of the pomegranate again suggests. The anguished interrogation at the end of II seeks to break through these limitations and to soften the silence which exists. In III love is seen again as unexpressed, here by the refusal of the beloved person to infuse the relationship with life and communication. The poet sees himself as dead and finds the same death in the lack of expressed love.

The third segment of the poem is composed of the following four *décimas,* all of which revolve around the interplay of the contradictory absence and presence of the beloved:

IV

Te alejas de mí pensando
que me hiere tu presencia,
y no sabes que tu ausencia
es más dolorosa cuando
la soledad se va ahondando,
y en el silencio sombrío,
sin quererlo, a pesar mío,
oigo tu voz en el eco
y hallo tu forma en el hueco
que has dejado en el vacío.

V

¿Por qué dejas entrever
una remota esperanza,
si el deseo no te alcanza,
si nada volverá a ser?
Y si no habrá amanecer
en mi noche interminable
¿de qué sirve que yo hable
en el desierto, y que pida,
para reanimar mi vida,
remedio a lo irremediable?

VI

Esta incertidumbre oscura
que sube en mi cuerpo y que
deja en mi boca no sé
qué desolada amargura;
este sabor que perdura
y, como el recuerdo, insiste,

y, como tu olor, persiste
con su penetrante esencia,
es la sola y cruel presencia
tuya, desde que partiste.

VII

Apenas has vuelto, y ya
en todo mi ser avanza,
verde y turbia, la esperanza
para decirme: "¡Aquí está!"
Pero su voz se oirá
rodar sin eco en la oscura
soledad de mi clausura
y yo seguiré pensando
que no hay esperanza cuando
la esperanza es la tortura. (pp. 80-81).

In each stanza the figure of the beloved is distant from the poet; in each there is contradictory mitigation and agitation of the anguish brought about by that absence. In IV, for example, the beloved has gone but the poet finds indication of reality in the empty forms which have been left behind. In V the separation is an emotional one, in which the poet laments the mere presence of a remote hope that the distance between can be overcome. In VI, the poet has a bitter sense of desolation and solitude, and in VII the merest suggestion of a return causes a painful and turbulent flourishing of hope.

Décimas VIII and IX make up the fourth structural segment of the poem:

VIII

Ayer te soñé. Temblando
los dos en el goce impuro
y estéril de un sueño oscuro.
Y sobre tu cuerpo blando
mis labios iban dejando
huellas, señales, heridas...
Y tus palabras transidas
y las mías delirantes
de aquellos breves instantes
prolongaban nuestras vidas.

IX

Si nada espero, pues nada
tembló en ti cuando me viste

y ante mis ojos pusiste
la verdad más desolada;
si no brilló en tu mirada
un destello de emoción,
la sola oscura razón,
la fuerza que a ti me lanza,
perdida toda esperanza,
es... ¡la desesperación! (p. 81).

These two *décimas* represent the dark and sterile dream of a desperate love. In VIII the poet brings his beloved to life in the figuration of a dream, and in the very act of expressing love leaves only wounds which have a symbolic quality. The delirious emotion on the part of the poet and the brief utterances on the part of the beloved seem to prolong this existence, but still in the unreality of the dream. In IX the situation is continued, and the poet realizes that there is no responding emotion in the eyes nor the being of his beloved, and he feels impelled only by the same desperate search for love and communication.

The fifth segment is composed of the final *décima* of the poem, which is a counterbalance to the first and introductory stanza:

X

Mi amor por ti ¡no murió!
Sigue viviendo en la fría,
ignorada galería
que en mi corazón cavó.
Por ella desciendo y no
encontraré la salida,
pues será toda mi vida
esta angustia de buscarte
a ciegas, con la escondida
certidumbre de no hallarte. (p. 82).

This final segment is an affirmation of continuing love, in spite of its impossible condition and the irrevocable absence of the beloved. The poet's emotion is alive in the cold expanse of his being, and he continues to search for the pathway which leads him toward life and a communication of his love. At the same time, however, he realizes with a sense of blind anguish that he will never be able to realize this possibility, and is condemned to search eternally without recompense.

The careful structuring of the thematic development of the poem, as well as the equally balanced and exact syntactical and metrical development of each of the individual *décimas,* makes this poem a successful representation of the peculiar love theme in Villaurrutia's poems.

A somewhat different aspect of the theme is presented by the composition "Amor condusse noi ad una morte": [4]

> Amar es una angustia, una pregunta
> una suspensa y luminosa duda;
> es un querer saber todo lo tuyo
> y a la vez un temor de al fin saberlo.
>
> 5 Amar es reconstruir, cuando te alejas,
> tus pasos, tus silencios, tus palabras,
> y pretender seguir tu pensamiento
> cuando a mi lado, al fin inmóvil, callas.
>
> Amar es una cólera secreta,
> 10 una helada y diabólica soberbia.
>
> Amar es no dormir cuando en mi lecho
> sueñas entre mis brazos que te ciñen,
> y odiar el sueño en que, bajo tu frente,
> acaso en otros brazos te abandonas.
>
> 15 Amar es escuchar sobre tu pecho,
> hasta colmar la oreja codiciosa,
> el rumor de tu sangre y la marea
> de tu respiración acompasada.
>
> Amar es absorber tu joven savia
> 20 y juntar nuestras bocas en un cauce
> hasta que de la brisa de tu aliento
> se impregnen para siempre mis entrañas.
>
> Amar es una envidia verde y muda,
> una sutil y lúcida avaricia.
>
> 25 Amar es provocar el dulce instante
> en que tu piel busca mi piel despierta;

---

[4] The title is a line from Dante's *Inferno* (Canto V, line 106) in which Francesca laments her physical and spiritual death. In an unpublished study, Donald Bevelander has considered the possible significance of the title for Villaurrutia and the dantesque structuring of this poem in terms of the capital sins, in particular anger, envy, avarice, and lust.

saciar a un tiempo la avidez nocturna
y morir otra vez la misma muerte
provisional, desgarradora, oscura.

30   Amar es una sed, la de la llaga
     que arde sin consumirse ni cerrarse,
     y el hambre de una boca atormentada
     que pide más y más y no se sacia.

     Amar es una insólita lujuria
35   y una gula voraz, siempre desierta.

     Pero amar es también cerrar los ojos,
     dejar que el sueño invada nuestro cuerpo
     como un río de olvido y de tinieblas,
     y navegar sin rumbo, a la deriva:
40   porque amar es, al fin, una indolencia. (pp. 76-77).

This is not one of the poems in which there is a considerable amount of metrical or syntactical freedom, but rather a sense of connection and organization. There is a systematic strophe pattern and a relationship of quatrain to couplet, and as well the line length is hendecasyllabic. Perhaps the greatest sense of connection, however, comes from the anaphoric use of the verb "amar" in each of the stanzas in succession.

The central theme of the poem is a consideration of the nature of love, suggested by the repetition of the infinitive form, and is developed in four segments. Each of the segments has the same structure: a specific statement of various aspects of the *yo — tú* love relationship, followed by an abstract statement related to one or more of the capital sins. For example, the first segment (lines 1-10) is composed of two quatrains which make up the specific statement and a closing couplet which is the abstraction. Love is, this segment suggests, anguish, questioning, doubting, and the reconstructing, both in the absence and presence of the beloved, of those small things which go to make up the reality of a person. The couplet, without any direct mention of the beloved, suggests that the act of loving is both passionate anger and cold and calculating pride.

The same alternating pattern between quatrain and couplet is to be seen in the following two structural segments. The second (lines 11-24) is made up of three quatrains which suggest a very close physical relationship between the two lovers. The poet keeps watch

over his sleeping beloved, and is aware of life and movement which
only he can see. The poet also feels the effects of his awareness in
those moments in which intimate physical contact is made. The closing
couplet again reduces these particularized stanzas to an abstraction.
The act of loving is an envy which flourishes as a silent plant and an
avarice which is sharp and clear. Segment three (lines 25-35) differs
slightly in metrical form in that the first stanza has five lines rather
than the four which have been the pattern up to this point. However,
the thematic development is the same. Love is represented here as
reaching an emotional climax, but never really being fulfilled. The
couplet again makes the abstraction: the act of loving is a lust which
is never satisfied.

The final segment of the poem (lines 36-40) is made up of the
final five lines of the poem. There is no closing couplet here, but
the structural pattern is the same. The first four lines of the stanza
represent the act of loving as dreaming, as floating down a shadowy
river of forgetfulness, without direction or particular purpose, and the
final line is the abstraction: the act of loving is after all else indolence.

In this poem the relationship between lover and beloved is not
one of absence or distance, but rather one of contact and emotional
climax. The act of loving, together with the need for love and communication, is repeatedly made the axis of the poem. However, the
recurring abstraction toward the capital sins creates an overriding
sensation of guilt in the relationship between the two beings, and love
is filled with a sense of anguish and doubt.

Still another example of the theme of love can be seen in the
"Soneto del temor a Dios":

> Este miedo de verte cara a cara,
> de oír el timbre de tu voz radiante
> y de aspirar la emanación fragante
> de tu cuerpo intangible, nos separa.
>
> ¡Cómo dejaste que desembarcara
> en otra orilla, de tu amor distante!
> Atado estoy, inmóvil navegante,
> ¡y el río de la angustia no se para!
>
> Y no sé para qué tendiendo redes
> con palabras pretendo aprisionarte,
> si, a medida que avanzan, retrocedes.

Es inútil mi fiebre de alcanzarte,
mientras tú mismo, que todo lo puedes,
no vengas en mis redes a enredarte. (p. 85).

The careful hendecasyllables and the *abrazado* rhyme scheme make this a perfect classical sonnet in form, and the equally careful oppositions developed throughout are very reminiscent of Sor Juana Inés de la Cruz and other earlier figures of the Spanish barroque period.

Tomás Segovia suggests that this poem is indicative of a return to religious themes which the poet had not used since his earliest works.[5] The title suggests immediately a love poem "a lo divino," and the strong *yo — tú* relationship in the sonnet can be seen as the gulf between suffering man and distant deity. The first quatrain suggests an unbridgeable chasm between the two, in which the features, voice, and fragrance of the divine being can only be imagined. The second quatrain laments this separation, questions the reason for man's separation from God, and recognizes the difficulties and anguishes of man's existence. The two tercets develop, in succeedingly intricate oppositions, the desire on the part of man to reach out toward divinity, and the inevitable impossibilities of such an attempt. The image of the net is suggestive in this context of similar imagery recorded in the New Testament in some of the parables of Christ and actions of some of his disciples.

As is usually the case with poetry "a lo divino," an interpretation in terms of worldly love is just as acceptable. The forces and uncertainties of "amor mundano" can just as well be the motivating impulse behind the anguished and impassioned *yo — tú* relationship. The poet is separated from his beloved and must imagine a face, the sound of a voice, and the fragrance of an untouchable and distant person. The poet laments the action of the beloved, which has forced him to live in complete separation, inextricably bound and immobilized in a flow of anguish. The verbal nets which he throws out to imprison anew his beloved are useless, because the beloved continues to withdraw from him. Only by an impossible act of love will the poet finally be able to encompass his beloved as he so ardently desires.

------

[5] Segovia, "Xavier Villaurrutia," *op. cit.,* p. 62.

Death

The theme of death differs from the other two major themes already considered in this chapter, in that its development is confined mainly to *Nostalgia de la muerte*. The consideration of the theme, therefore, will take up only compositions from that collection.

The theme of death is not always developed in the same fashion, but is represented in some poems as a presence which pervades the surroundings, in others as a process which affects the poet inevitably in his circumstance, and in others as a personification which also has an intimate relationship with the poet. Perhaps the best example of the first of these facets is the composition "Nocturno de la alcoba," in which death takes on the multiple forms which the poet sees in the room in which he finds himself:

> La muerte toma siempre la forma de la alcoba
> que nos contiene.
>
> Es cóncava y oscura y tibia y silenciosa,
> se pliega en las cortinas en que anida la sombra,
> 5   es dura en el espejo y tensa y congelada,
> y profunda en las almohadas y, en las sábanas, blanca.
>
> Los dos sabemos que la muerte toma
> la forma de la alcoba, y que en la alcoba
> es el espacio frío que levanta
> 10   entre los dos un muro, un cristal, un silencio.
>
> Entonces sólo yo sé que la muerte
> es el hueco que dejas en el lecho
> cuando de pronto y sin razón alguna
> te incorporas o te pones de pie.
>
> 15   Y es el ruido de hojas calcinadas
> que hacen tus pies desnudos al hundirse en la alfombra.
>
> Y es el sudor que moja nuestros muslos
> que se abrazan y luchan y que, luego, se rinden.
>
> 20   Y es la frase que dejas caer, interrumpida.
> Y la pregunta mía que no oyes,
> que no comprendes o que no respondes.
>
> Y el silencio que cae y te sepulta
> cuando velo tu sueño y lo interrogo.

25 Y solo, sólo yo sé que la muerte
es tu palabra trunca, tus gemidos ajenos
y tus involuntarios movimientos oscuros
cuando en el sueño luchas con el ángel del sueño.

La muerte es todo esto y más que nos circunda,
30 y nos une y separa alternativamente,
que nos deja confusos, atónitos, suspensos,
con una herida que no mana sangre.

Entonces, sólo entonces, los dos solos, sabemos
que no el amor sino la oscura muerte
35 nos precipita a vernos cara a cara a los ojos,
y a unirnos y a estrecharnos, más que solos y náufragos,
todavía más, y cada vez más, todavía. (pp. 60-61).

The form of the poem is generally free, with no specific pattern of line length, stanza, or rhyme. There is a very definite division into stanzas, however, and there is a considerable amount of non-systematic assonance throughout the poem. The central theme of the poem is the omnipresence of death and its ability to take on the shapes and essences of things which surround the poet. There is a consistent *yo — tú* relationship which is reminiscent of the love poems already commented on, but used here to provide a kind of double reflection for the pervasive presence of death.

The poem can be divided into three developmental segments. The first of these segments is composed of the first three stanzas (lines 1-10), and develops the basic relationships and direction of the entire composition. Death takes the form of the bedroom in which the poet and his beloved find themselves, and conforms itself to the shapes and sounds of the room. It has curvature, color, warmth, reflection, and hardness, as the situation demands. Both the poet and his beloved recognize this multiplicity of forms, and know that death erects between them a silent and crystalline wall which separates them from each other.

The second segment includes the following six stanzas (lines 11-28). Here the point of view shifts from the duality of the *yo — tú* to the singleness of the *yo*. The poet realizes also that many of the things which he associates with the presence of his beloved also speak of death: a hollow which indicates the previous presence of the beloved, the sound of bare feet on the floor, the warmth of a sexual

embrace, and the interrupted phrases and questions which remain
unanswered. This segment of the poem is very highly connected by
a series of verbs and conjunctions which operate in an anaphoric
fashion to suggest the meanderings of the poet's mind as he considers
these matters.

The final two stanzas of the poem (lines 29-37) make up the third
major segment of the poem, and serve as a kind of recapitulation of
those elements which have gone before. Death is all the many things
which the poet passes before his consciousness, and this all-encompassing presence separates and unifies the poet and his beloved at the
same time. The realization of this presence leaves them confused
and expectant, as well as deeply wounded. The two at that moment,
together but alone at the same time, realize that their experience is
not one of love entirely but rather of a common tasting of the presence
of death which throws them more closely together. The contradictory
ambiguousness of the final lines, with the impossible interfacing of
intimacy and shipwreck, heighten the anguish and ambiguity of this
all-encompassing presence.

In other poems of the collection death is seen as an inevitable
process. "Muerte en el frío" is probably the best example:

> Cuando he perdido toda fe en el milagro,
> cuando ya la esperanza dejó caer la última nota
> y resuena un silencio sin fin, cóncavo y duro;
>
> cuando el cielo de invierno no es más que la ceniza
> 5 de algo que ardió hace muchos, muchos siglos;
>
> cuando me encuentro tan solo, tan solo,
> que me busco en mi cuarto
> como se busca, a veces, un objeto perdido,
> una carta estrujada, en los rincones;
>
> 10 cuando cierro los ojos pensando inútilmente
> que así estaré más lejos
> de aquí, de mí, de todo
> aquello que me acusa de no ser más que un muerto,
>
> siento que estoy en el infierno frío,
> 15 en el invierno eterno
> que congela la sangre en las arterias,
> que seca las palabras amarillas,
> que paraliza el sueño,

que pone una mordaza de hielo a nuestra boca
20 y dibuja las cosas con una línea dura.

Siento que estoy viviendo aquí mi muerte,
mi sola muerte presente,
mi muerte que no puedo compartir ni llorar,
mi muerte de que no me consolaré jamás.

25 Y comprendo de una vez para nunca
el clima del silencio
donde se nutre y perfecciona la muerte.
Y también la eficacia del frío
que preserva y purifica sin consumir como el fuego.

30 Y en el silencio escucho dentro de mí el trabajo
de un minucioso ejército de obreros que golpean
con diminutos martillos mi linfa y mi carne estremecidas;

siento cómo se besan
y juntan para siempre sus orillas
35 las islas que flotaban en mi cuerpo;

cómo el agua y la sangre
son otra vez la misma agua marina,
y cómo se hiela primero
y luego se vuelve cristal

40 y luego duro mármol,
hasta inmovilizarme en el tiempo más angustioso y lento,
con la vida secreta, muda e imperceptible
del mineral, del tronco, de la estatua. (pp. 66-68).

It can be seen at once that although there is clear division into strophes and consistent punctuation that the poem has considerable freedom in its form. The lines are largely conventional (predominantly heptasyllables, hendecasyllables, and Alexandrines), but there is no consistent arrangement into strophes. There is no fixed rhyme scheme, although there is scattered assonance throughout the poem, in particular in á-o in the second half.

The principal theme of the composition is that of inevitable death as a process, and this theme is developed in three principal structural parts. The first of these is made up of the first five strophes (lines 1-20). The first strophe is an extensive dependent clause in which an auditory image suggests the sensation of desperateness and resounding silence, a sense impression which is augmented by aspects of hardness and visual form. A second suspended clause follows the first, and the winter sky, now gray and ashen, is added to the previous silence and lack of hope. The two following strophes (lines 6-14), each in the same syntactical form, relate a state of solitude to the silent wintry panorama. The poet has no identity, and he must close his eyes in order to escape from himself and from the silence of his own existence. Three run-on lines (10-13) produce two extensive syntactic periods arranged around the particle "de mí," and underline the anonymity and solitude of the poet's internal state. A fifth strophe (lines 14-20) is the syntactical resolution of the previous strophes, and is at the same time a summary and a thematic extension. The first two lines make apparent, principally by means of thermic images, the frigid inferno of the poet. The word play "invierno — infierno" (lines 14-15) suggests intensity and amplitude. The four following verses (16-19) describe in parallel constructions the effects of this icy desolation: the processes of the physical body are suspended and the means of communication is closed off. The final line of the strophe shows that the spectral images of silence and solitude are to be seen everywhere.

Strophes 6 and 7 (lines 21-29) constitute the second structural part of the poem. Here the silent and desperate isolation of winter becomes the environment in which life is changed into solitary and unlamented death. The thermic images continue to function: cold and silence do not consume as do fire and passion, but rather preserve the superficial appearance of life.

The final three strophes (lines 30-43) form the third structural division of the composition, and here the process which takes life toward death is represented and experienced. In the eighth strophe the poet realizes that he is living material, shaped by a host of diminutive workers who possibly can represent the numerous small actions of life which determine the reality of our existence. In the ninth strophe the circulation of the blood is suspended and in the tenth strophe the transformation is completed. The body fluids congeal, then crystallize, and finally become marble. The poet thus is left immobile, silent and mineral-like in a suspended and anguished temporal dimension. The thermic images are combined here with auditory impressions of silence and noisy hammering as well as tactile and lapidary suggestions in order to communicate the anguished thematic resolution of the whole poem.

In other poems of the collection death is personified, at times as nothing more than a shadowy figure ("Para darme muerte/la muerte esperaba", p. 48) and at other times as a woman with whom one has had a long and familiar relationship. "Nocturno en que habla la muerte" is probably the best example of this view of death:

Si la muerte hubiera venido aquí, a New Haven,
escondida en un hueco de mi ropa en la maleta,
en el bolsillo de uno de mis trajes,
entre las páginas de un libro
5   como la señal que ya no me recuerda nada;
si mi muerte particular estuviera esperando
una fecha, un instante que sólo ella conoce
para decirme: "Aquí estoy.
Te he seguido como la sombra
10   que no es posible dejar así nomás en casa;
como un poco de aire cálido e invisible
mezclado al aire duro y frío que respiras;
como el recuerdo de lo que más quieres;
como el olvido, sí, como el olvido
15   que has dejado caer sobre las cosas
que no quisieras recordar ahora.
Y es inútil que vuelvas la cabeza en mi busca:
estoy tan cerca que no puedes verme,
estoy fuera de ti y a un tiempo dentro.
20   Nada es el mar que como un dios quisiste
poner entre los dos;
nada es la tierra que los hombres miden
y por la que matan y mueren;
ni el sueño en que quisieras creer que vives
25   sin mí, cuando yo misma lo dibujo y lo borro;
ni los días que cuentas
una vez y otra vez a todas horas,
ni las horas que matas con orgullo
sin pensar que renacen fuera de tí.
30   Nada son estas cosas ni los innumerables
lazos que me tendiste,
ni las infantiles argucias con que has querido dejarme
engañada, olvidada.
Aquí estoy, ¿no me sientes?
35   Abre los ojos; ciérralos, si quieres."

Y me pregunto ahora,
si nadie entró en la pieza contigua,
¿quién cerró cautelosamente la puerta?
¿Qué misteriosa fuerza de gravedad

40 hizo caer la hoja de papel que estaba en la mesa?
    ¿Por qué se instala aquí, de pronto, y sin que yo la invite,
    la voz de una mujer que habla en la calle?

    Y al oprimir la pluma,
    algo como la sangre late y circula en ella,
45 y siento que las letras desiguales
    que escribo ahora,
    más pequeñas, más trémulas, más débiles,
    ya no son de mi mano solamente. (pp. 54-55).

The poem is divided into three stanzas of unequal length in which
there is also no pattern of metrical length or of end rhyme. There
is however some scattered assonance, as in a number of other poems
of this collection, and notably frequent run-on lines.

The theme of the poem is the omnipresence of death, and the
impossibility of escaping it no matter how far the poet may travel.
The reference to New Haven in line 1 suggests that here again the
poem was at least conceived during the time the poet was in the United
States and thus removed from his customary surroundings. It is possible to see the development of the central theme in two segments.
The first of these is made up entirely by the first long stanza, which
represents an imaginary confrontation between the poet and a personified death. A series of verbs in the imperfect subjunctive prepare
for the utterance of personified death. "If my own private figure of
death were here with me, waiting for the proper moment to reveal
herself", muses the poet and then constructs for himself the words
she might say. Even though she cannot be seen or touched, death
observes that it is impossible for the poet to leave her behind or to
erase her from his consciousness. Death continues to surround him
and at the same time be deeply within him.

The second part of the poem is made up of the final two strophes
(lines 36-48), and brings the poet back to reality. Yet, certain things
seem to happen which are beyond his control, and which suggest an
unknown presence. A door closes, a paper falls to the floor, a woman's
voice is heard within the room, and as the poet writes a mysterious
power affects the letters which flow from his pen. Here the actions
are expressed in present and past indicative; the poet no longer has
to suppose the presence of accompanying death: she is with him,
revealing herself through many small circumstances.

Another and more complex example is to be found in "Décima muerte," one of the poet's best known compositions. Here again, as in the previously discussed "Décimas de nuestro amor," the poet chooses the carefully worked *décima* form in ten stanzas.

The *yo* — *tú* relationship which has been seen in many of the other poems is here also the principal vehicle for the development of the theme. There is a constant exchange between the poet's anguished awareness of himself as the *yo* and the shadowy and overwhelming presence of death as the *tú*. This contradictory relationship, developed through the careful *décima* stanzas, can be seen in four developmental segments. The first of these, made up of the first three *décimas*, can be seen as an attempt to describe this relationship:

I

¡Qué prueba de la existencia
habrá mayor que la suerte
de estar viviendo sin verte
y muriendo en tu presencia!
Esta lúcida conciencia
de amar a lo nunca visto
y de esperar lo imprevisto;
este caer sin llegar
es la angustia de pensar
que puesto que muero existo.

II

Si en todas partes estás,
en el agua y en la tierra,
en el aire que me encierra
y en el incendio voraz;
y si a todas partes vas
conmigo en el pensamiento,
en el soplo de mi aliento
y en mi sangre confundida,
¿no serás, Muerte, en mi vida,
agua, fuego, polvo y viento?

III

Si tienes manos, que sean
de un tacto sutil y blando,
apenas sensible cuando
anestesiado me crean;
y que tus ojos me vean

sin mirarme, de tal suerte
que nada me desconcierte
ni tu vista ni tu roce,
para no sentir un goce
ni un dolor contigo, Muerte. (pp. 70-71).

In the first stanza, life and existence can be explained by the unrealized search for death which the poet insists upon. The awareness of loving something which has not been seen yet and expecting the unexpected, causes the poet to reflect in anguish that the only proof of his existence is the process toward death. The second *décima*, which is very reminiscent of both Góngora and Sor Juana Inés de la Cruz, sees death as an elemental part of life. Death is so much a part of him and the things around him that he must reflect, in the final two lines of the stanza, that death or personified death is for him as important as the four principal elements were for ancient man.

Décima III exists in the form of a request, expressed in a series of subjunctive verbs. The poet, in view of the intimate relationship between himself and personified death, requests that her touch be barely felt, as if he were anaesthetized or unaware of other sense impressions.

The following two *décimas* change the focus of the poem slightly:

IV

Por caminos ignorados,
por hendiduras secretas,
por las misteriosas vetas
de troncos recién cortados,
te ven mis ojos cerrados
entrar en mi alcoba oscura
a convertir mi envoltura
opaca, febril, cambiante,
en materia de diamante
luminosa, eterna y pura.

V

No duermo para que al verte
llegar lenta y apagada,
para que al oír pausada
tu voz que silencios vierte,
para que al tocar la nada
que envuelve tu cuerpo yerto,

para que a tu olor desierto
pueda, sin sombra de sueño,
saber que de ti me adueño,
sentir que muero despierto. (p. 71).

In both of these stanzas the figure of death enters the bedroom of the poet, and in a dream-like sequence he sees that certain things will occur at that particular moment. In IV, for example, death enters his room in a number of small and secret ways, perhaps again indicative of the almost imperceptible progress of death in life, and is able to convert his existence into something resembling the hardness and luminosity of a diamond. In V the poet lies awake in order to watch the slow and silent arrival of death, and by reaching out to the contradictory silences and emptinesses of death, is able to be more deeply aware of that process.

The third segment is made up of *décimas* VI-VIII, which depend on a physical relationship between the *yo* of the poet and the personified death figure:

VI

La aguja del instantero
recorrerá su cuadrante,
todo cabrá en un instante
del espacio verdadero
que, ancho, profundo y señero,
será elástico a tu paso
de modo que el tiempo cierto
prolongará nuestro abrazo
y será posible, acaso,
vivir después de haber muerto.

VII

En el roce, en el contacto,
en la inefable delicia
de la suprema caricia
que desemboca en el acto,
hay un misterioso pacto
del espasmo delirante
en que un cielo alucinante
y un infierno de agonía
se funden cuando eres mía
y soy tuyo en un instante.

VIII

¡Hasta en la ausencia estás viva!
Porque te encuentro en el hueco
de una forma y en el eco
de una nota fugitiva;
porque en mi propia saliva
fundes tu sabor sombrío,
y a cambio de lo que es mío
me dejas sólo el temor
de hallar hasta en el sabor
la presencia del vacío. (p. 72).

In VI the moment of death is likened to a lover's embrace, and the poet contemplates the extension of this embrace in his obsessive musings on death. Perhaps in this way, the poet indicates, he will be able to achieve death in life and thereby a kind of life after death. VII continues the figure of a lover's embrace in more intensity and detail, and contemplates death as something which can be represented in the caresses and even the spasms of physical love. However, this love and awareness are momentary, and therefore extremely hallucinatory and anguished. In stanza VIII the physical relationship is only suggested, here as absence and echo and emptiness, but nonetheless physical in the suggestion of the image of saliva. The poet fears that in return for his surrender of himself in the lover's embrace with the figure of death that he will find only the same emptiness which has characterized his life.

The fourth part is one of summation, and is made up of the last two *décimas* of the poem:

IX

Si te llevo en mí prendida
y te acaricio y escondo;
si te alimento en el fondo
de mi más secreta herida;
si mi muerte te da vida
y goce mi frenesí,
¿qué será, Muerte, de ti
cuando al salir yo del mundo,
deshecho el nudo profundo,
tengas que salir de mí?

X

En vano amenazas, Muerte,
cerrar la boca a mi herida
y poner fin a mi vida
con una palabra inerte.
¡Qué puedo pensar al verte,
si en mi angustia verdadera
tuve que violar la espera;
si en vista de tu tardanza
para llenar mi esperanza
no hay hora en que yo no muera! (p. 73).

Décima IX is a summarized recognition of the intimacy and anguish of the *yo — tú* relationship which has been developed. The poet carries with him at all times the figure of death, and continues to nourish it within the most intimate part of his being. At the same time, however, he questions Death directly as to what will happen at that moment when he really dies. Since his anguish gives pleasure and his death will give life in the sense of being freed from his embrace, the poet then wonders about the continued existence of this particular and peculiar figuration which he has contrived.

Décima X exists as a challenge to the personified death figure. Her silence, the poet says, does not frighten him nor can it really put an end to his existence. If death approaches, as he sees that it does, his intense anguish in life gives him at least one satisfaction: death has no real power over him since there has not been a time in which his life has not been a living death. He no longer fears death because he has met her, embraced her, and becomes one with her many times before.

The development of "Décima muerte," with its careful metrical patterns, its neo-baroque plays of precise counterposition, and its insistent development of a personified death, lead to one final example which is a fitting close to the consideration of this theme in Villaurrutia's poems. This composition, with the title of "Epitafio," [6] expresses with finality the idea of multiple experiences of death in a contradictory state of life:

---

[6] There is some indication that Villaurrutia intended this as a real epitaph, but it is curious to realize that at the time of his death his family and his friends had inscribed on his tomb another epitaph, also included in his poetic works, which was evidently dedicated to Jorge Cuesta.

II

Duerme aquí, silencioso e ignorado,
el que en vida vivió mil y una muertes.
Nada quieras saber de mi pasado.
Despertar es morir. ¡No me despiertes! (p. 90).

Minor Themes

In addition to the main themes already discussed in this chapter,
there are several minor thematic threads which appear intermittently
throughout Villaurrutia's poems, and need to be considered separately
here. Poetry and poetic creation, nature and the peaceful life, and
religious experience are all themes which appear in some poems,
particularly in the very early and the last collections, and there are
some compositions which are related thematically to Villaurrutia's
travel in the United States. None of these is insistent enough to
warrant discussion as a primary focal point of the poet's verses, but
each should be considered briefly.

The theme of poetic creation is first used by Villaurrutia in a
very early poem, "Le pregunté al poeta...," which is very reminiscent
of some early Modernist verses:

Le pregunté al poeta su secreto
una tarde de lloro,
de lluvia y de canción,
y me dijo el poeta: "Mi secreto
no lo dictan los sabios en decreto.
En la orilla del Nilo y en la aurora
interroga a Memnón..."

Le pregunté al poeta su secreto
una noche de luna,
una noche de augurios y de mal.
El poeta me contestó con una
mirada que era un reto
y me dijo: "Interroga
a la estatua de sal..."

Yo descansé la frente entre las manos
(un grupo de aves emprendió la huida).
Mis preguntas y anhelos eran vanos,
el poeta callaba su secreto
porque era ese secreto el de su vida. (pp. 4-5).

The poem takes the form of an imagined dialogue between the young and inexperienced *yo* and "el poeta," who already knows the secret of life. On several occasions the voice of inexperience questions, but instead of receiving answers is commanded to turn to Memnon or the Biblical statue of salt. The questions and concerns are all in vain, since the poet can no more explain the process of poetry than he can explain the reasons for his own existence.

In "Poesía," the composition which now opens *Reflejos,* the poet finds himself immersed in the mystery of the words and the processes of poetry. The words which spring from the deep well of his being form a personification, whose hand takes control of the creative process ("Tu mano metálica . . . conduce la pluma/que traza en el papel su litoral.", p. 26) and whose external form is as a mirror in which the poet can view himself ("y en tu piel de espejo/me estoy mirando mirarme . . .", p. 26). However, these structures are so fragile that the slightest sound will destroy them, and the poet again finds himself deserted ("y me dejas/sin más pulso mi voz y sin más cara,/sin máscara como un hombre desnudo/en medio de una calle de miradas.", p. 26). In this composition the poet seems to emphasize, rather than the mystery and secret of poetry, its essential impossibility and fragileness.

In "Palabra," a composition that appeared posthumously, the poet personifies the poetic word and assigns to her regal qualities of pride and mystery:

> Palabra que no sabes lo que nombras.
> Palabra, ¡reina altiva!
> Llamas nube a la sombra fugitiva
> de un mundo en que las nubes son las sombras. (p. 85).

Here the word itself, rather than the poet or poetry as indicated in the previous two compositions, is the focus for the mystery of poetic creation. The word in its personified regal form can express in a single figure the complex and subterranean reality which stands behind it, in this case the relationship being nube = sombra = mundo fugitivo (nubes = sombras).

The poet's development of this theme is not extensive, as can be seen from these examples, but there is enough of a development to underscore sharply the poet's interest in the expressiveness of language and the mystery of poetic creation.

Villaurrutia cannot in any way be characterized as a religious poet; his principal themes lead strongly in the direction of immediate physical experience. However, there are several poems in which religious experience becomes the dominant thematic focus. Most of these are to be found in *Primeros poemas* ("Plegaria," "Breviario," "Ya mi súplica es llanto"), and probably the best example is "Ni la leve zozobra":

> Mi corazón, Señor, que contiene el sollozo,
> que palidece y deja sin rumbo su latir,
> mi corazón huraño y misericordioso
> se te da como un fruto maduro de sufrir.

> Mi corazón, Señor, hermética granada
> de un resignado huerto donde no llega el
> luminar de cielo de la casta mirada,
> ni la antorcha perenne de la palabra fiel.

> Se abandona al saber que tu milagro quedo
> enterrará el afán, el presagio y el miedo,
> y el más íntimo engaño ahogará desde hoy.

> Porque el dolor tenaz sustituirá un aroma,
> y desde la oblación que a tu quietud se asoma,
> ni la leve zozobra temblará en lo que soy... (p. 20).

This composition, a sonnet which differs slightly from the classical metrical pattern, takes the form of a lament in which the poet recognizes the depths of his suffering and at the same time the miracle which will remove pain and fear. The quatrains of the sonnet express the suffering felt by the poet, and use the figure of the pomegranate to symbolize the heart hidden from any of the mitigating effects of divine power. The tercets take the opposite aspect, and in spite of the suffering already expressed, there is a recognition of a quiet miraculous power which will touch the most distant part of the poet's being. This poem uses many of the same symbols which become familiar in the later works of the poet, but here the emphasis is on a release from pain and suffering, rather than on the anguish which becomes apparent in later compositions.

The poet does not continue with this theme in *Reflejos* or in *Nostalgia de la muerte,* and it is only taken up momentarily again in the posthumous composition "Soneto del temor a Dios." This

sonnet has been discussed in detail already in this chapter, and needs
be mentioned here only as a closing point for this minor theme.

A third minor theme which appears from time to time in the two
earlier collections but which disappears entirely in *Nostalgia de la
muerte* and *Canto a la primavera,* is that of a peaceful life in bucolic
surroundings. For example, "En el agua dormida" from *Primeros
poemas* develops in careful Alexandrine quatrains a peaceful scene
in which the poet exists without anxiousness or anguish at any time:

> En el agua dormida mi caricia más leve
> se tiende como el perro humilde de la granja;
> la soledad en un impalpable oro llueve,
> y se aclara el ambiente oloroso a naranja.
>
> Las pupilas, alertas al horizonte puro,
> interrogan sin rumbo, sin anhelo ni angustia,
> cada sombra cobija un cansancio futuro
> que doblega la frente en una flexión mustia.
>
> En tanto, un inefable candor que nada implora
> es descanso a los ojos ... Escucho un trino huraño,
> y pienso inversamente que a una nube viadora
> guía el pastor bíblico conduciendo el rebaño.
>
> En un temblor de seda se deshoja la hora,
> ni un súbito reflejo turba el agua dormida,
> ni un cansancio impaciente en mi alma se desflora,
> ni la vida me siente, ni yo siento la vida ... (p. 21).

The scene developed in the poem is that of a peaceful summer's
afternoon in which all of the senses find joy and comfort: the gold
of the sunlight, the sound of a bird, the smell of orange blossoms,
and the calm surface of the water. The striking image of the first
stanza, in which the poet's caress (perhaps his glance) on the still
water is compared to the reclining shape of the farmyard dog, adds
to the visual quality of the poem. Also, the pastoral suggestion made
in the third stanza increases the sense of bucolic peace, and heightens
as well the visual impression of clouds tumbling one on top of
another. Amidst all these elements of calm and peace, the poet finds
himself in the same state of emotion: he does not feel upset or hurried
and is satisfied with simply being.

An example from *Reflejos* is the composition "Domingo," in which the poet imagines a Sunday's journey into the country:

Me fugaría al pueblo
para que el domingo
fuera detrás del tren
persiguiéndome . . .

Y llegaría en la tarde
cuando, ya cansado
el domingo, se sentara
a mi lado,
frente al paisaje
quieto,
bajo los montes
que tampoco se habrían rasurado.

Así podría yo tenderme
sin hastío.
Oír sólo el silencio,
y mirar el aire incoloro
y poroso.

Muy abajo, muy pequeño,
junto al domingo
fatigado,
siguiendo la sola nube:
¡Dios fuma tras de la montaña! (p. 34).

The composition takes the form of an imagined journey away from the town, a journey which is conditioned by a series of verb tenses in the imperfect subjunctive and conditional and as well by a curious personification of Sunday. The poet longs to flee and would have the personified Sunday follow behind him. Upon their arrival, both tired, they would be able to sit quietly and contemplate the scenery before them. They would both sit underneath trees made shaggy by leaves and vegetation, or as the image of the second stanza suggests, still "unshaven". In that way the poet would simply be able to exist, to listen to the silence and be aware of the transparent atmosphere. His contemplations make him feel small, and as he watches the movements of the clouds he wonders if they are not produced by some superhuman being (God is the word the poet uses but seemingly without any religious reference) who is smoking behind the mountain. Here again the development of theme and imagery seems to reduce any sense of anguish to nothingness and to increase the feeling of pleasurable existence within peaceful surroundings.

The compositions in which Villaurrutia uses situations from his trip to the United States represent a separate thematic grouping. In other poems already discussed, there have been occasional references to place names and situations, but in two compositions this becomes a primary thematic focus. The first of these, "North Carolina Blues," is a take-off on the jazz music of the time and is dedicated to Langston Hughes, the American Negro poet. The poem has an unusual structure, in that it is made up of eight segments of varying length, each of which is followed by the refrain line "En North Carolina." These elements all have to do with Villaurrutia's reaction to the situation of the black man in North Carolina and the United States. For example, the first strophe captures the tragedy in a drop of sweat:

> En North Carolina
> el aire nocturno
> es de piel humana.
> Cuando lo acaricio
> me deja, de pronto,
> en los dedos,
> el sudor de una gota de agua.
>
> *En North Carolina* (p. 65).

Stanza 6 reveals in separate waiting rooms the absurdity of this kind of separation:

> En diversas salas de espera
> aguardan la misma muerte
> los pasajeros de color
> y los blancos, de primera.
>
> *En North Carolina* (p. 66).

Stanza 7 is the culmination of the poem. Here Villaurrutia perceives the entire situation as nightmarish, a nocturnal hotel in which things move by themselves and into which invisible couples (invisible because they are dark) enter. A disembodied hand, as if it were the hotel attendant receiving guests, writes and erases black names on the blackboard, which again suggests invisibility and even insanity:

Nocturnos hoteles:
llegan parejas invisibles,
las escaleras suben solas,
fluyen los corredores,
retroceden las puertas,
cierran los ojos las ventanas.
Una mano sin cuerpo
escribe y borra negros
nombres en la pizarra.

En North Carolina (p. 66).

The second composition in which this same thematic organization functions is the gathering of short satiric verses on Boston which are entitled "Epigramas de Boston." There are eight numbered sections of widely varying length and organization, but all with the purpose of poking fun at the puritanism and conventionality of Bostonians. In strophe 1, for example, Bostonians dress so much alike that they might as well be nudists:

I

El puritanismo
ha creado
un nuevo pecado:
el exceso de vestido,
que, bien mirado
y por ser tan distinguido,
en nada se distingue del nudismo. (pp. 87-88).

Even arquitecture is acceptable only when it is traditional:

IV

Como los rascacielos
no son tradicionales,
aquí los ponen por los suelos,
horizontales. (p. 88).

The desire for superficial morality is so strong, the poet affirms, that men and women must have separate exits from hotels and elevators and at the same time must find secret ways to meet far from the public gaze:

VI

En hoteles y ascensores
la moral consabida
exige diferente salida
a las damas y a los señores.

De modo que los maridos,
los amantes, los pretendientes
y los recién casados
tienen que estar pendientes
para reunirse, de manera
subrepticia y privada,
con la esposa, la amada,
la novia o la niñera. (p. 89).

The puritanical condemnation of passion is so great that even the poet is reluctant to mention certain fallen women, and must create a verbal play in order to express himself:

VIII

En Boston es grave falta
hablar de ciertas mujeres,
por eso aunque nieva nieve
mi boca no se atreve
a decir en voz alta:
ni Eva ni Hebe. (p. 89).

CHAPTER VI

EVALUATIONS AND CONCLUSIONS

General

The preceding chapters of this study develop an internal view of the poetry of Xavier Villaurrutia which is structured on a scale of increasing complexity. The fundamental considerations of lexicon and syntax lead directly into a discussion of metrical form. The study of imagery takes into account the material already presented, and at the same time adds greater explicative depth and variety. The examination of major and minor themes is based primarily on explications of a number of complete texts, and is in a sense the culmination of the whole process of internal study.

The discussions in this final chapter will present an external view, and in the form of recapitulation and judgment will consider both Villaurrutia's poetry in its own terms and the poet's place as a national and international literary figure. The first problem to be treated will be the complex question of influence, and then an evaluation of Villaurrutia's total production will be proposed. The final segments of the chapter will have to do with the placement of the poet within Mexican literature and as a part of a literary tradition which goes beyond national boundaries.

Influence and Originality

A glance at Villaurrutia's critical essays is sufficient to show that he did not write in isolation, but rather was aware of and was in a very real sense a part of the broad currents of Western artistic

expression. His notes en such disparate figures as Ramón López Velarde, Sor Juana Inés de la Cruz, Jorge Luis Borges, Paul Valéry,
Pío Baroja, Elmer Rice, Walt Whitman, Jean Giraudoux, Jean Cocteau, Rainer María Rilke, and Luigi Pirandello display wide and
sensitive readings as well as the propensity to use such readings in
relationship to his own creative work.

At the same time, however, it is not possible to characterize
Villaurrutia as surrealistic, impressionistic, neo-Baroque, or Imagistic.
The essential fact is that Villaurrutia was not orthodox in anything.
Tomás Segovia suggests, in support of this lack of orthodoxy, that
the poet's work was uniquely his own, and that whatever he took
from sources that he shared with his contemporaries became a part
of his peculiar structuring of reality.[1] I do not propose a detailed
influence study here, but as a preamble to an evaluation of Villaurrutia's poetry it seems appropriate to consider briefly the important
influences which helped to shape the peculiar world of the poet.

Early Influences

The two poetic presences most at hand for Villaurrutia and the
other young poets of his group were Enrique González Martínez, as
a transitional figure of late Modernism, and Ramón López Velarde,
as an original new voice in the expression of Mexican reality.

González Martínez was the father of Enrique González Rojo, one
of the young poets of the "Contemporáneos" group, and consequently
was a paternal figure for them all. Villaurrutia has commented, for
example, that while he had profound respect for González Martínez'
poetry he felt compelled not to use as a model for his own.[2] This
assertion is an overstatement of the truth, however, because a number
of Villaurrutia's early poems show an unmistakable trace of González
Martínez' attitude of calm profundity:

> El agua, que en el pozo paralizó sus ansias,
> dijo con sus cristales virtudes olvidadas,
> como nuestras abuelas en las viejas estancias,
> con los ojos abiertos y las manos cansadas.

---

[1] "Xavier Villaurrutia," *Revista Mexicana de Literatura* (Núm. 16-18, oct.-dic. de 1960), 54-55.
[2] "Ramón López Velarde," *Obras*, p. 642.

Y así, suspensa el alma por la emoción divina,
el ayer de la vida no fue claridad vana,
y supo el corazón lo que punza una espina . . .
Ayer, bajo el sigilo de la luna lejana.

("Bajo el sigilo de la luna," *Primeros
poemas*, p. 21).

Villaurrutia documents an early familiarity with López Velarde's
Zozobra,[3] and even describes some few meetings with the poet in the
National Preparatory School. Villaurrutia does not confess any great
debt to López Velarde, but at the same time some of the rural scenes
and striking metaphors of various early poems are strongly reminiscent
of the older poet. In the following lines, for example, an audacity of
imagery is combined with a sharp awareness of a typical Mexican
scene:

Aquel pueblo se quedó soltero,
conforme con su iglesia,
embozado en su silencio,
bajo la paja —oro, mediodía—
de su sombrero ancho,
sin nada más:
en las fichas del cementerio
los + son —.

("Pueblo," *Reflejos*, p. 34).

Villaurrutia saw the French symbolists as a much more important
early influence on his work, something that could be received and
used without any shred of remorse: "Yo escribía versos en que los
simbolistas franceses, Albert Samain sobre todos, dejaban su música,
su atmósfera y no pocas veces sus palabras. . . . La influencia más
remota e imprecisa la aceptaba sensualmente, como quien recibe una
vaga emanación, un perfume lejano."[4] A number of compositions in
Primeros poemas show this influence clearly, and the following
quatrains make a particularly good example:

La tarde deslizóse lentamente
como barca en un lago de aguas quietas,
en tu pecho temblaron las violetas
acariciadas por un soplo ardiente.

---

[3] *Ibid.*, p. 641.
[4] *Ibid.*, p. 642.

Allí te murmuré junto a la fuente,
en el parque que guarda ansias secretas,
"Yo soy como el minero que las vetas
de tu cariño ansía reverente . . ."

("Como barca en un lago . . . ," p. 3).

Another significant influence, seen most evidently in *Reflejos,* is that of the Impressionist painters. Albert Lopes notes, for example, a relationship in technique between Villaurrutia and Cézanne:

El interés que manifiesta Villaurrutia por la pintura es muy evidente en estos poemas [*Reflejos*]. En el verso hace lo que hizo el inimitable pintor francés, Cézanne, en la pintura de "naturaleza muerta." Para los dos, el objeto está modelado de tal manera que parece concreto a la mente, pero al mismo tiempo, es más atractivo a causa de la detallada descripción . . . [5]

The repeated use of the frame, the reflected image, and the still-life pose are all indications of the considerable influence of the Impressionists on Villaurrutia at that moment. However, it is an exaggeration to see *Reflejos* only as a collection of objective word paintings. A much more profound emotional state is immediately visible beneath the surface description:

Paisaje inmóvil de cuatro colores,
de cuatro limpios colores:
azul, lavado azul de las montañas
y del cielo,
verde, húmedo verde en el prado
y en las colinas,
y gris en la nube compacta,
y amarillo.

Paisaje inmóvil de cuatro colores
en torno mío
y en el agua.
¡Y yo que esperaba

---

[5] "La poesía de Xavier Villaurrutia," *Memoria del Segundo Congreso Internacional de Catedráticos de Literatura Iberoamericana* (Berkeley and Los Angeles, 1941), p. 252.

hallar, en el agua siquiera,
el mismo incolor que en mi alma!

("Incolor," p. 39).

Later Influences

Tomás Segovia proposes three major influences on Villaurrutia's poetry: Rilke's concept of death, Heidegger's idea of Nothingness, and the subconscious dream techniques of Surrealism. [6] To these might be added that of the early Italian surrealist Giorgio de Chirico. Let us look at each in turn.

The importance of the theme of death for Villaurrutia has caused a number of critics, in addition to Segovia, to mention in passing the importance of Rainer María Rilke in the development of that theme. Alí Chumacero, for example, mentions briefly Rilke's peculiar view of death in life and its relationship to Villaurrutia's poetry. [7] Elías Nandino recognizes Rilke as the source for some of Villaurrutia's ideas on a personal death. [8] Frank Dauster finds only a slight relationship between the two poets. [9] The only extended consideration of this influence, however, is an unpublished study by Lía Schwartz de Lerner, entitled "Rilke y Villaurrutia: estudio de una influencia," which serves as the principal source for my comments.

Points of contact between the work of the Austrian poet and Villaurrutia are not constructs on the part of critics, but are based on the Mexican's own comments. In 1940, for example, Villaurrutia wrote the prologue for the publication in Mexico of a Spanish translation of Rilke entitled *Melodía del amor y muerte del corneta Cristóbal Rilke*. [10] In that prologue, which now appears in the *Obras* volume under the title of "Rainer María Rilke," the Mexican poet makes plain an early and enduring familiarity with the poetry of Rilke:

> La lectura de la traducción francesa de *Los cuadernos de Malte Laurids Brigge* fue mi primer encuentro con la

---

[6] "Xavier Villaurrutia," p. 55.

[7] "Prólogo," *Obras de Xavier Villaurrutia* (México, FCE, 1966), p. xv.

[8] "La muerte en la poesía de Xavier Villaurrutia," *Cuadernos de Bellas Artes*, No. 5 (dic. de 1960), 7-10.

[9] *Xavier Villaurrutia* (New York, Twayne, 1971), p. 113.

[10] México, Ed. Letras de México, 1940. Traducción de E. García Máynez y prólogo de Xavier Villaurrutia.

> obra de Rainer María Rilke. Encuentro definitivo, imborra-
> ble y no superado después de la lectura de cuantas obras de
> Rilke, traducidas al francés, he tenido en mis manos. ¿Quiere
> esto decir que *Los cuadernos de Malte Laurids Brigge* es la
> mejor obra de Rilke? Sería inconsecuente afirmarlo. Las
> *Cartas a un poeta* y *Los cuadernos de Malte Laurids Brigge*
> son las obras de Rilke que, por lo visto, resisten mejor a la
> traducción. Ni los famosos *Sonetos a Orfeo,* ni las *Elegías de
> Duino,* ejemplares por la finura de su lenguaje, por el ritmo
> y la música originales, me han vuelto a dar, leídas en francés,
> el estremecimiento angustioso, misterioso y nostálgico de *Los
> cuadernos.* (p. 949).

On another occasion Villaurrutia again made reference to Rilke,
but this time not by name:

> Descubro, pues, la aparición del tema de la muerte. ¿Por
> qué? Acaso porque en momentos como los que ahora vivimos
> la muerte es lo único que no le pueden quitar al hombre; le
> pueden quitar la fortuna, la vida, la ilusión, pero la muerte
> ¿quién se la va a quitar? Si la muerte la llevamos, como
> decía un poeta, dentro, como el fruto lleva la semilla. Nos
> acompaña siempre, desde el nacimiento, y nuestra muerte
> crece con nosotros. ("Introducción a la poesía mexicana,"
> p. 771).

The phrase "como decía un poeta" is obviously a reference to Rilke
and indirectly to one of his fundamental concepts.

These citations from Villaurrutia himself would seem to make
appropriate and necessary a consideration of the question.

Mrs. Lerner makes three fundamental points in discussing what
she feels to be a legitimate literary influence. First, by his own admis-
sion, Villaurrutia read Rilke only in French translation, and not in
the original German. Therefore, stylistic and formal considerations
are not appropriate, and the influence can be limited to a tracing of
the ideas of death and solitude (p. 2). Second, Villaurrutia uses some
aspects of the theme of death as found in Rilke, such as personal
death and the fear of oncoming death, but these concepts are not
wholly like Rilke (p. 2). Third, some points of contact are visible —
the use of the theme of solitude, but here again Villaurrutia does not
follow Rilke's ideas completely (p. 17). Mrs. Lerner's conclusion on
these matters seems to sum up succinctly the whole question:

Nuestro autor ha encontrado en el poeta de las *Elegías de Duino* algunas ideas que incorpora a su poesía. Pero en la elaboración de ellas crea algo nuevo que no es copia sino manifestación de sus propias experiencias y recreación artística. En otras palabras, Villaurrutia no sigue a Rilke en su visión del mundo ni en las últimas consecuencias de su ideario; Villaurrutia más bien aprovecha la posibilidad poética de ciertas afirmaciones rilkeanas y las incorpora sin coherencia y asistemáticamente. No se trata de adopción sino de adaptación. (p. 10).

A possible influence of Martin Heidegger on Villaurrutia's poetry is more difficult to establish. Here again the point of departure is a statement by the poet himself, but in this case a much less detailed one which is open to various interpretations. The poet's only mention of Heidegger is found in the 1940 interview with José Luis Martínez and Alí Chumacero, and is recorded as follows:

—¿Qué significación, más bien, qué intención le daría Ud. a su libro "Nostalgia de la Muerte?"
—En él aparecen dos temas que son capitalmente interesantes para mí: la muerte y la angustia. La angustia del hombre ante la nada, una angustia que da una peculiar serenidad.
—¡Heidegger!
—Sí. Todo poeta descubre su filósofo y yo lo he encontrado en Heidegger. Pero el descubrimiento del sentido, del tono de mi poesía, no lo he tenido tan fácilmente. Hubo un día en que me di cuenta de que entendía particularmente *el clima de la noche,* el del *Nocturno,* que era como la clave para mi poesía, y dentro del *Nocturno* la muerte. Si una característica esencial tiene para mí el hombre moderno —lo he dicho ya en algún periódico— es la de morir y asistir a su propia muerte. La vive auténticamente todos los días —yo al menos— y tiene la posesión de la angustia, del misterio. [11]

In addition to Segovia's brief comment, already noted above, several other critics have made mention of this point of contact. Miguel Capistrán, for example, considers the matter very briefly, [12]

---

[11] "Con Xavier Villaurrutia," *Tierra Nueva* (marzo-abril, 1940), p. 78.
[12] "Ulises, Simbad, Villaurrutia o la curiosidad," *Revista de Bellas Artes,* No. 7 (enero-febrero 1966), 6-38.

and Frank Dauster gives more important attention to it both in his 1953 article on Villaurrutia's poetry and in his recent book. Dauster's principal argument is that Villaurrutia's statement indicates that his poetry and thought were formed before his contact with Heidegger's ideas: "We have Villaurrutia's express statement [in the 1940 interview with J. L. Martínez] that although he felt Heidegger to be the philosopher closest to his own preoccupations, he had formulated the body of his thought before reading Heidegger for the first time." [13] A shorter unpublished study by Richard A. Valdés centers on the possible relationship between Heidegger and Villaurrutia, and takes exception with Dauster's interpretation of the poet's statement. He points out, for example, that Villaurrutia's comment in the interview is almost a word-for-word rendering of a statement from *What is Metaphysics*: "It would be truer to say that dread is pervaded by a peculiar kind of peace" [14] ("La angustia del hombre ante la nada, una angustia que da una peculiar serenidad", p. 15).

The principal difficulty in the whole matter is that in accordance with the sketchy information available, there is no way to determine when and in what circumstances Villaurrutia may have read Heidegger. Valdés examines translations into French and Spanish prior to 1940, and can make only the following inconclusive assertion: "From this we can draw the conclusion that by 1932 . . . Villaurrutia could have become aware of the philosophy of Heidegger, at least in a general way" (p. 13).

There do seem to be some unassailable points of comparison. Dauster mentions them briefly: "There are certain obvious similarities, such as the interest in the relations between time and existence, the stress or anguish and the effort to comprehend the nature of death" (p. 109). Valdés goes into greater detail in an effort to justify influence. For example, he sees the idea of dread of Nothing as peculiar to Heidegger and seen often enough in Villaurrutia's poetry to be beyond the realm of coincidence. The composition "Volver" with its constant mention of "la nada," is, according to Valdés, ". . . the

---

[13] *Xavier Villaurrutia*, p. 109.
[14] "What is Metaphysics? (Was ist Metaphysik)," translated by Hull and Crick in *Existence and Being*, edited by Werner Brock (Chicago, Regnery, 1949), p. 328.

clearest example of the Heideggerian idea of Nothing in the poetry
of Villaurrutia" (p. 27). [15]

What conclusion is to be drawn then from the information
available? Dauster's conclusion that Villaurrutia's use of time, anguish,
and death "was adopted independent of foreign influences" (p. 109)
is too extreme. Rilke's part in these ideas is too clear, and though
less discernibly, the poet certainly made use of certain of Heidegger's
fundamental philosophical ideas.

The matter of the influence of Surrealism on Villaurrutia is even
more complex. Prior to 1935, while the movement was still in its
early stages, Villaurrutia had written several critical essays on early
European figures, [16] and he continued this critical attention during
the following decades. However, at no time did he say clearly that
he felt himself influenced by the movement, its theories, or its major
figures.

Perhaps the most important documentation of an early contact
with Surrealism is a short "escritura automática" which carries a date
of 1929: [17]

> Se habla, a menudo, de la escritura automática mediúmnica
> Lenormand en ese acto Carmela charla con l'otra y la pluma
> no sirve ya raja cola de secante a mi izquierda el puño de
> la camisa me queda largo el ruido de cristales estrépito
> de plaza que se oye afuera y ya oigo lo que dicen azul y
> con una línea Agustín Lazo y las mujeres que bordan el
> estambre de mi corbata la risa la tos acabe ya entiendes
> Santa Teresa me detengo sin pensar en nada es imposible
> otra vez la uña descuidada Ermilo y sus copias punto curioso
> la firma que rompe la pluma y la muñeca que se cansa
> Pellicer que no trae los poemas me duele más que la muñeca
> aquel chiquillo no me gusta es absurdo todo esto fluye y se
> encima la taquigrafía lo remediaría nada nada noche no sé
> lo que voy a escribir todo lo que hago es inconscientemente

---

[15] This composition was one of the last things written by the poet, and
appeared only after his death. Could it be that Heidegger's importance for
Villaurrutia is to be seen in the post-1940 period, rather than in earlier years?

[16] See, for example: "Paul Morand," *Revistas de Revistas*, 13 de febrero
de 1927; "En torno de Jean Giraudoux," *El Universal Ilustrado*, 19 de
junio de 1924; "La rosa de Cocteau," *Número*, otoño de 1933.

[17] This piece, a part of a fragmentary diary in the unmistakable hand
of the poet, was first published in *Estaciones*, II (Núm. 6, verano de 1957),
pp. 138-140, and appears in *Obras* on p. 618.

absurdo ya no puedo más el trazo sobre el aire la madera
estriada tríada es triada de cristal y laca plomo blanco y
papel. (p. 618).

As Tomás Segovia points out, this text reveals an awareness of
Surrealism, but at the same time it shows the characteristic Villaurrutia adaptation. [18] The technique is surrealistic, and the elements are
peculiar to the poet himself: proper names, emotions, references to
small surrounding details, and even a play on words "la madera
estriada tríada es triada de cristal y laca...". Segovia goes on to
make strongly again the case for Villaurrutia's individuality in using
any outside material:

> Tal vez es ésta la razón de que Villaurrutia, como casi
> todos los poetas de lengua española, por otra parte, tomara
> del surrealismo lo que buenamente le convino tomar, sin con-
> vertirse nunca en ortodoxo, y poniendo las ganancias hurtadas
> a esta escuela al servicio de su personal expresión, que no
> hay que confundir con una inconsciente expresión. Villaurru-
> tia tomó simplemente cierta atención hacia el sueño y su
> procedimiento, que utiliza en la creación sólo por analogía
> y no literalmente, y también las ventajas de cierta libertad
> que él no llevó nunca hasta el abismo de la gratuidad.
> (p. 55).

The same lack of orthodoxy can be seen plainly in the poet's
application of surrealistic technique in his own work. As Segovia
observes (p. 56), and as I have pointed out in an earlier chapter,
Villaurrutia never follows any system (or lack of system) completely.
In those poems in which the metrical system tends toward the free
associative flow of the subconscious (for example, "Nocturno amor"
or "Nocturno en que habla la muerte") the imagery and theme
development are consciously clear and organized. On the other hand,
in those poems in which imagery and conception might be considered
nearer Surrealism (for example, "Nocturno sueño" or "Nocturno de
la estatua") metrical form and punctuation control are again clear
and often systematic. At the same time, the generalization just expressed has its own exceptions as well. "Nocturno en que nada se
oye" seems to me to be as close as Villaurrutia comes to a surrealist

---

[18] Segovia, p. 55.

poem, both from the point of view of metrics as well as imagery and theme. The same might be said, though probably a bit reduced in scale, of "Nocturno de los ángeles." Again, in spite of somewhat fragmentary evidence from the poet himself, it seems clear that while Villaurrutia is not a surrealist any more than he is an existentialist, the lessons learned from Surrealism and put to use in his own work are clear and important.

Villaurrutia does mention, however, another figure that should be taken into account in assessing the effect of Surrealism on his works: "Es curioso, quizá existan en mi obra, más que influencias de algunos escritores, la de un pintor. En Chirico encontré muchas veces una clara afinidad en esa manera de evasión de las cosas." [19] A rather early contact with De Chirico can be docuemented in the reproductions and commentaries which appeared in *Contemporáneos.* [20]

The poet's words are sufficiently vague so as to make precise specification of influence rather difficult. However, there do seem to be points of contact between De Chirico's faceless figures in endless repetitions of shadows, walls, and streets and such verses as these from Villaurrutia:

> ¿Y quién entre las sombras de una calle desierta,
> en el muro, lívido espejo de soledad,
> no se ha visto pasar o venir a su encuentro
> y no ha sentido miedo...
>
> ("Nocturno miedo," *Nostalgia de la muerte,* p. 45).

James H. Soby calls De Chirico's forms "more dreamlike than real," infused with an enigmatic light which at times "casts no shadows, seeming to make the objects it illuminates apparitional; at other times ... it casts distorted shadows of invisible bodies." [21] Perhaps it is this sense of imprecision and mystery that the poet sees as so much akin to his own work. At any rate, it would seem appropriate to include the painting of De Chirico among the important influences which helped to shape Villaurrutia's mature poetic work.

---

[19] "La poesía," *Revista de Bellas Artes,* Núm. 7 (enero-febrero de 1966), 17-19. This material does not appear in *Obras.*
[20] See, for example, the reproductions of several paintings under the title "Telas" (I, 3, agosto de 1928, 265-271).
[21] *The Early Chirico* (New York, 1941), p. 80.

Evaluation

This section of the study will attempt an external evaluation of the various collections of the poet, without special regard for sequences of thematic development of techniques. I will give attention to both collections and individual poems.

Primeros poemas

There is no way to view the poems collected under this title in an organic way, since this arrangement was made by the editor of Villaurrutia's poems after his death. The principal components are the twelve compositions which appeared as a part of the anthology *Ocho poetas* (México, 1923); the remaining poems appeared in a variety of journals from 1919 to 1923.

All of the poems grouped under this title are easily seen as poems of adolescence. As has already been noted in this chapter, early influence is at times overpowering, and in only a few instances are individual compositions able to stand alone as convincing artistic entities. For example, the sentimentality and stylized imagery of many compositions ("En la tarde que muere"; "Le pregunté al poeta"; "Plegaria"; "Lamentación de primavera") seem overly dependent on Modernism, and the passion and intended symbolism of others ("El viaje sin retorno"; "El"; "Canción apasionada") are too intense to be persuasive. On the other hand, there are three or four excellent poems, which give notice of a real poet beneath the apprentice's baggage. "Variaciones de colores," "Esta música," and "Tarde," three poems published when the poet was only 17 years old, [22] make unstilted use of novel sensorial imagery, and do not have the insistent juvenile emotional transports which characterize most of the other compositions. "Antes," which was published for the first time in 1923, [23] expresses, in an unusual metaphor comparing the heart and a house, a youthful ardor and candor which are doomed to pass:

---

[22] "Variaciones de colores" was first published in *Policromías* (Núm. 14, mayo de 1920), "Esta música" in *Aurora* (1920), and "Tarde" in *El Monitor Republicano* (3 de octubre de 1920). Only "Tarde" reappeared in the 1923 anthology *Ocho poetas*.

[23] This poem appeared both in *El Heraldo de la Raza* (Núm. 24, 15 de agosto de 1923) and in *Ocho poetas* (México, Porrúa, 1923).

Aún no tenía la casa arrugas,
ni cicatrices, ni temor.
Otro día ... (p. 19).

Reflejos

Villaurrutia's first book of poems was published in 1926 under the title of the opening composition, "Reflejos." [24] Though some early influences are still visible, I see in its 35 short pieces some of the poet's most successful work. The rhetoric of youth has been tempered, and increasing individuality dominates.

There are several elements which work together harmoniously toward a favorable judgment. First, the poems are vividly sensorial. A face reflected on the surface of the water, a still life, landscapes seen from an open window, a record player, the roofs of houses seen starkly against the sky, or the shaded intricacies of a formal garden are all caught and communicated by the careful flow of language. The visual functions together with the auditory, the thermic, and the tactile to represent successfully and unpretentiously the vivid scenes desired by the poet.

Second, there is at the same time a strong sense of the unusual in these poems. Metrical form is never conventional, and the poems take a free-flowing shape which is simple but obviously under the poet's control. At the same time, the imagery is often surprising and never extravagant. The peaches in a still life, for example, are represented as having a "piel de quince años", and the distant sound of a train whistle becomes the chilling sound of chalk being drawn figuratively across the blackboard of childhood memory.

Finally, there is a surprising profundity of meaning to be found beneath the limpid surface of the poems. Solitude stares out from the eyes of a feminine figure painted on canvas, the instant of love is surrounded by an endless night of insomnia and fatigue, life is to be seen with a contradictory sense of immobility and hurried journeyings, time slips away in the ticking of a clock or the beating of a human heart, and the poet thirsts after a renewed clarity of vision:

---

[24] As previously indicated the composition "Poesía," which now appears in the *Obras* as the first poem, was not published until 1927. Only four of the compositions had appeared previously ("Soledad"; "Cuadro"; "Cézanne"; "Pueblo"), and some eight or nine were re-published separately afterward, largely in journals outside Mexico.

Tengo sed.
¿De qué agua?
¿Agua de sueño? No.
De amanecer.

("Agua," p. 43).

Nostalgia de la muerte

This collection, probably Villaurrutia's most substantial and characteristic *poemario,* evolved over more than a decade. Several poems in the *nocturno* form appeared as early as 1928 and 1929 in the pages of *Contemporáneos,* and were later reprinted separately under the title of *Nocturnos* (1933). These texts were combined with some other *nocturnos* and later *nostalgias* (including five stanzas of "Décima muerte") in the first edition of *Nostalgia de la muerte* (Buenos Aires, Sur, 1938). The remaining stanzas of "Décima muerte", together with another *nocturno,* were published in *Décima muerte y otros poemas no coleccionados* (México, Nueva Voz, 1941), and were incorporated finally in the definitive edition, *Nostalgia de la muerte* (México, Mictlan, 1946).

This is a far more somber collection of poems than *Reflejos.* The passing reflections of a placid world have disappeared, and the anguished sense of death, solitude, and incoherence, seen only fitfully in *Reflejos* beneath the calm surface of some of the poems, is now the overpowering view.

The nineteen *nocturnos,* grouped under two headings in the final edition of the collection, are together probably the most important part of Villaurrutia's mature poetry. Youthful enthusiasms have vanished, and the reflected multiplicity of the world has been reduced to a single aspect: dark, silent, subterranean, and bitter. Metrical form in these poems is generally open, and the corresponding flow of language is in keeping with the themes and emotions represented. The plasticity of poetic language tends to be reduced in comparison to that of *Reflejos,* and the thematic development of the poems is insistent, at times repetitive. These poems are no longer brilliant sensorial flashes with a hint of profundity, but are rather a long and painful incursion into the shadowy meanings of the poet's own existence, and by extension, of human existence. Many, if not all, of the *nocturnos* are successful as poetry because they engage and involve the reader in those meanings.

EVALUATIONS AND CONCLUSIONS

Four of the five compositions grouped under the title of "Nostalgias" are to a certain extent occasional poems, in that they are connected at least in part with the poet's visit to the United States. Two poems represent Villaurrutia's contradictory impressions of the snow, which he undoubtedly experienced for the first time in New Haven: these two are of moderate interest, though the chromatic interplay never justifies them entirely. A better poem is "Muerte en el frío," in which the process of death is seen in terms of thermic contrasts. "North Carolina Blues," a series of interconnected sketches using as a basis the black man in the American South, is successful only in the representation of some striking images.

"Décima muerte" is included as the fifth poem under the title of "Nostalgias," and is far more important than the other texts in that section. This poem is one of Villaurrutia's major representations of the theme of death, and proceeds in carefully measured periods toward a characteristic humanized figure of death. The theme is carefully structured, and the balanced complexities of imagery and language carry the poem along toward the conclusion which is inevitable from the beginning. From the point of view of emotion, however, the composition is less convincing. The poet mentions anguish and death, but his carefully turned neo-baroque circles are almost too perfect. I do not deny the artistry of "Décima muerte," but simply affirm that for me the profundities of death and solitude are more meaningfully expressed in some of the *nocturnos*.

Canto a la primavera y otros poemas

As early as 1941, Villaurrutia had in mind a series of love poems: "el poema ... es el primero de una improbable pero no imposible serie de poemas amorosos que si es verdad que supe cuando dió principio, no sé cuando la continuaré, ni siquiera si la continuaré." [25] In 1948 Villaurrutia was awarded a prize for his composition "Canto a la primavera," and the series of love poems which had been under way for some years were published together with the prize-winning composition the same year. [26]

---

[25] Prologue to *Décima muerte y otros poemas no coleccionados* (México, Nueva Voz, 1941).

[26] The 1966 *Obras* edition adds six poems which were not a part of the original publication: "Deseo," "Palabra," "Soneto del temor a Dios," "Crepuscular," "Estatua," "Epigramas de Boston."

The poems of this collection contain the most concentrated expression of one of the major themes of the poet, and as such communicate successfully the anguish and suspense of unrealized love. In technique and imagery, these poems tend to be less complex than those of preceding collections, and the metrical forms are in general more traditional. However, the emotional intensity of these compositions has not diminished.

Of the ten poems published in the original edition, two seem to me to be particularly good. "Soneto de la granada" is one of Villaurrutia's best. Its carefully turned phrases and images express within the limits of the sonnet the mysteries and realities of Villaurrutia's poetic world, and at the same time the impossibility of their being communicated completely. The contradictory impossibilities of love are expressed particularly well in "Amor condusse noi ad una morte."

Some of the other poems of the collection are less convincing. For example, "Canto a la primavera" seems to be in some ways a set piece in which the stanzas express the theme of renovation but in which the cliché of spring is never entirely overcome. "Nuestro amor" develops imperfectly the theme of tormented and doubting love, and resolves itself almost as a game: "¡no fuera amor el nuestro, no fuera nuestro amor!"

The longest and most ambitious poem of the collection is "Décimas de nuestro amor," which is obviously based on the previous "Décima muerte." [27] Here again each *décima* is directed toward an intensified personification, not the figure of death but rather of the beloved person whose presence is ardently desired. This composition has the same strong points and the same limitations as "Décima muerte." The representation of the theme is intricate and careful, and the language used is polished and multifaceted in keeping with the thematic development. However, this very intricacy and perfection do not support entirely the desperate emotions intended, and I am again inclined to see these *décimas* as a rather abstract handling of an emotional subject.

---

[27] Only 3 *décimas* were published in the 1948 edition of *Canto a la primavera* (these now appear as stanzas 2, 3, and 10 of the final version of the poem), and the entire poem was published posthumously in *Cuadernos Americanos*, enero-febrero, 1951.

Xavier Villaurrutia and Mexican Literature

As a preamble to his 1940 interview with Villaurrutia, José Luis Martínez makes the following assertion as to the poet's place in contemporary Mexican literature: "Si hemos buscado esta comunicación con el poeta de los *nocturnos,* ello se debe, más que a una afinidad y estimación de su obra que no sería sino una personal razón, al hecho de su significación preponderante en el campo de la literatura mexicana contemporánea." [28] This favorable estimate of Villaurrutia was due in part to his compelling personality and wide literary relationships. For example, Celestino Gorostiza affirms that "Xavier Villaurrutia ... representaba entre nosotros la elegancia espiritual, el ingenio incisivo y la rápida agudeza ..." [29] and Rodolfo Usigli points out the poet's generosity in aiding others in their writing: "Tenía una curiosidad infatigable, un ingenio inagotable, y uno de sus mayores placeres era trabajar con otros escritores haciéndoles ver las faltas en que habían incurrido o la forma en que podían mejorar lo que habían escrito." [30] Frank Dauster documents several concrete examples in which the poet's personality and wit can be seen in the works of several younger writers, particularly Beltrán, Chumacero, and Carballido. [31]

Villaurrutia's approach to artistic creation was consistently an esthetic one, and his name is consequently often used in the discussions of the need for local as opposed to universal values in Mexican literature. Frank Dauster defends Villaurrutia against "the charges of anti-Mexicanism", and finds that his poetry is "rooted firmly in the tradition of his people and his nation ...". [32] It is certainly true that Villaurrutia was more introspective than national in his view of poetic creation, but it is interesting to note that for many of the writers younger than Villaurrutia and his group it was precisely that sense of internal reality which they found attractive. For example, in an interview with the French critic Claude Couffon, Octavio Paz indicates that for him Villaurrutia and others of the "Contemporáneos" were

---

[28] "Con Xavier Villaurrutia," p. 74.
[29] *El trato con escritores, segunda serie* (México, Bellas Artes, 1964), p. 104.
[30] *Ibid.,* p. 169.
[31] *Xavier Villaurrutia* (New York, Twayne, 1971), p. 123.
[32] *Xavier Villaurrutia,* p. 122.

more important and more revolutionary than the so-called novelists of the revolution:

> A título de documentos, sus obras tienen una importancia capital. Pero para los escritores de mi generación, para mí, no abren ningún camino. Los poetas de esta época que se alejaron de la transcripción literal de la realidad ejercieron sobre nosotros una influencia mucho más vigorosa.
> —¿Se refiere, sin duda, a Carlos Pellicer y a José Gorostiza?
> —Sí y también a Xavier Villaurrutia. De hecho, Pellicer, Gorostiza y Villaurrutia fueron mucho más rebeldes que los novelistas de la revolución. A pesar de su indiferencia por la realidad inmediata, estaban, sin embargo, en el seno de la realidad; pero no la describían desde el exterior: la analizaban desde el interior, planteando de esta manera problemas de carácter moral. En lo que a mí respecta, me dieron la posibilidad de superarme y de encontrar insuficiente el mundo que me rodeaba. [33]

In addition to the aspects of the question already considered, it is important to see Villaurrutia as a part of Mexican literature through his own works of poetry. Alí Chumacero attempts this kind of judgment in his prefatory essay to *Obras*: "Nos dejó una obra poética no muy abundante, pero suficiente para que, al lado de nuestros más grandes poetas, se recuerde siempre su nombre." [34] Chumacero's guarded image of poetic immortality is one with which I would agree at this point. Xavier Villaurrutia is without doubt one of the several most important poetic voices in Mexican literature of the twentieth century, and in his insistent development of the anguished and lonely world within each man, must be given his place alongside Nezahualcóyotl, Sor Juana Inés de la Cruz, Manuel Díaz Mirón, Enrique González Martínez, and Ramón López Velarde in the full sweep of Mexican poetry.

Villaurrutia Outside Mexico

Xavier Villaurrutia is not found among the poets most cited in the current resurgence of interest in Latin American literature. His

---

[33] Claude Couffon, *Hispanoamérica en su nueva literatura* (Santander, Publicaciones la Isla de los Ratones, 1962), p. 75.
[34] *Obras*, p. xxii.

work is far more introverted and restrained than the pyrotechnics of a Huidobro, the committed Americanism of a Neruda, the ethnic magic of a Guillén, or the anguished hallucinations of a Vallejo. Nonetheless, Villaurrutia's unique view of his internal world contributes significantly to the totality of poetic expression in Latin America, and should be considered in this context.

In his recent history of Spanish American literature, Luis Leal includes Villaurrutia among those poets who best represent *vanguardista* style. [35] Though perhaps not one of the most important three or four figures, the poet's experiments with complexities of language, image, and metrical form, and his use of dream and chaotic mental flow in the representation of his peculiar poetic world make a substantial contribution to the poetry of his period. From a more biographical point of view, as well, Villaurrutia was very much aware of things going on in other countries of Spanish America, and had his material published in places as far away from Mexico as the River Plate region.

Outside the Spanish-speaking world, however, Villaurrutia is virtually unknown. Few of his works have been translated, and consequently he is not known to readers of English, French, or German. This might have come if the poet had lived longer, but at the moment it is not possible to accord Villaurrutia much more than a footnote-type mention in the history of world literature. And yet, as Tomás Segovia writes, he has much to say to those who can and are willing to listen:

> Quien crea que la poesía nada tiene que decirle a él, que se asome limpiamente a la obra de Villaurrutia, que se abra sin preconcebida mala fe, que la mire a los ojos, cara a cara, y la oiga murmurarle al oído, conmovedora e inquietante:
> Porque mi muerte es tu muerte ... [36]

---

[35] *Breve historia de la literatura hispanoamericana* (New York, Knopf, 1971), pp. 179-181.
[36] "Xavier Villaurrutia," p. 63.

INDEX TO POEMS STUDIED

Nostalgia de la muerte

INDEX OF NAMES

NORTH CAROLINA STUDIES IN THE ROMANCE LANGUAGES AND LITERATURES

I.S.B.N. Prefix 0-88438

Recent Titles

NORTH CAROLINA STUDIES IN THE
ROMANCE LANGUAGES AND LITERATURES

I.S.B.N. Prefix 0-88438

Recent Titles

FROM VULGAR LATIN TO OLD PROVENÇAL, by Frede Jensen. 1972. (No. 120). *-920-0.*

GOLDEN AGE DRAMA IN SPAIN: GENERAL CONSIDERATION AND UNUSUAL FEATURES, by Sturgis E. Leavitt. 1972. (No. 121). *-921-9.*

THE LEGEND OF THE "SIETE INFANTES DE LARA" (*Refundición toledana de la crónica de 1344* versión), study and edition by Thomas A. Lathrop. 1972. (No. 122). *-922-7.*

STRUCTURE AND IDEOLOGY IN BOIARDO'S "ORLANDO INNAMORATO," by Andrea di Tommaso. 1972. (No. 123). *-923-5.*

STUDIES IN HONOR OF ALFRED G. ENGSTROM, edited by Robert T. Cargo and Emmanuel J. Mickel, Jr. 1972. (No. 124). *-924-3.*

A CRITICAL EDITION WITH INTRODUCTION AND NOTES OF GIL VICENTE'S "FLORESTA DE ENGANOS," by Constantine Christopher Stathatos. 1972. (No. 125). *-925-1.*

LI ROMANS DE WITASSE LE MOINE. *Roman du treizième siècle.* Édité d'après le manuscrit, fonds français 1553, de la Bibliothèque Nationale, Paris, par Denis Joseph Conlon. 1972. (No. 126). *-926-X.*

EL CRONISTA PEDRO DE ESCAVIAS. *Una vida del Siglo XV,* por Juan Bautista Avalle-Arce. 1972. (No. 127). *-927-8.*

AN EDITION OF THE FIRST ITALIAN TRANSLATION OF THE "CELESTINA," by Kathleen V. Kish. 1973. (No. 128). *-928-6.*

MOLIÈRE MOCKED. THREE CONTEMPORARY HOSTILE COMEDIES: *Zélinde, Le portrait du peintre, Élomire Hypocondre,* by Frederick Wright Vogler. 1973. (No. 129). *-929-4.*

C.-A. SAINTE-BEUVE. *Chateaubriand et son groupe littéraire sous l'empire.* Index alphabétique et analytique établi par Lorin A. Uffenbeck. 1973. (No. 130). *-930-8.*

THE ORIGINS OF THE BAROQUE CONCEPT OF "PEREGRINATIO," by Juergen Hahn. 1973. (No. 131). *-931-6.*

THE "AUTO SACRAMENTAL" AND THE PARABLE IN SPANISH GOLDEN AGE LITERATURE, by Donald Thaddeus Dietz. 1973. (No. 132). *-932-4.*

FRANCISCO DE OSUNA AND THE SPIRIT OF THE LETTER, by Laura Calvert. 1973. (No. 133). *-933-2.*

ITINERARIO DI AMORE: DIALETTICA DI AMORE E MORTE NELLA VITA NUOVA, by Margherita de Bonfils Templer. 1973. (No. 134). *-934-0.*

L'IMAGINATION POETIQUE CHEZ DU BARTAS: ELEMENTS DE SENSIBILITE BAROQUE DANS LA "CREATION DU MONDE," by Bruno Braunrot. 1973. (No. 135). *-934-0.*

ARTUS DESIRE: PRIEST AND PAMPHLETEER OF THE SIXTEENTH CENTURY, by Frank S. Giese. 1973. (No. 136). *-936-7.*

JARDIN DE NOBLES DONZELLAS, FRAY MARTIN DE CORDOBA, by Harriet Goldberg. 1974. (No. 137). *-937-5.*

Symposia

LOS NARRADORES HISPANOAMERICANOS DE HOY, edited by Juan Bautista Avalle-Arce. 1973. (No. 1). *-951-0.*

When ordering please cite the *ISBN Prefix* plus the last four digits for each title.

Send orders to:

University of North Carolina Press
Chapel Hill
North Carolina 27514
U. S. A.